I PROBABLY SHOULDN'T have done THAT

I Probably Shouldn't Have Done That

Warning
This e-book contains adult language and may be considered offensive to some readers. Please store your files wisely, where they cannot be accessed by underage readers.

Copy Editor: Jessa Slade
Cover Artist & Layout Design: L.C. Chase
www.pickwickink.com
pickwickeditor@gmail.com general inquiries

ISBN: 978-0-9890979-3-2

I Probably SHOULDN'T have done THAT

To me.

Because if I don't dedicate a book to me, who the hell ever will? Crap. That sounds really egotistical. I probably shouldn't have done that. Shit.

TABLE OF CONTENTS

HELLO, MY NAME IS:

GENERAL WISDOM suggests you're supposed to live life without regrets.

Not me. I have some.

I try not to let them weigh me down and control my future decisions. Yet I sometimes enjoy touching those regrets in a friendly way, revisiting questionable decisions. Maybe I could have done something different. Maybe not. Maybe the resulting mess turned out absolutely perfectly.

Sometimes an awkward experience (*Flying High*) makes for a great story later. Maybe keeping silent during a homophobic moment (*Monsters*) strengthened my resolve to become a stronger advocate the next time. Maybe I'm a better man for the times I trusted strangers (*Faith in Bolinas*). Wondering about the questionable decisions I've made in life makes me who I am today.

I'm sure you made some questionable decisions. C'mon. Don't lie.

I don't trust people who don't have at least a few regrets. Did you not risk anything? Are you the careful master of making life turn out perfectly? I'm not suggesting we all run with scissors just to test the consequences and enjoy the random pleasure of having something to regret. I think the opportunity for making bad decisions comes up often enough without really courting disaster. Acknowledging my regrets and making them my teachers (and occasionally friends) is the only way I know to live with the decisions I've made.

I've made some choices you may not have made. And yeah, I often end up saying, "I probably shouldn't have done that." But isn't life more interesting for choosing the path more stupid? I included only twenty-five stories but I could have included a few dozen others. I may have to write a sequel titled, "I Probably Shouldn't Have Eaten That," followed by a collection of "I Probably Shouldn't Have Clicked Send."

Oh man. My name is Edmond Manning and I have done some really stupid things.

I hope you enjoy this collection my more questionable decisions. Perhaps you will see yourself in my antics. Maybe you can look at this as a cautionary tale. Either way, I am confident I will regret sharing some of these stories with the entire world. But, oh well. I'm used to having regrets.

FLYING HIGH

I KNEW as soon as I popped the candy into my mouth I had done something wrong.

Football Mom and Urban Cowboy's eyes bugged out in surprise and I realized I had somehow committed a serious airplane faux pas. Somehow.

True, I hadn't been listening to their spirited conversation for the past few minutes. I nodded occasionally when they included me, but the pilot had announced his intention to land our plane soonish and I very much wanted to finish reading my book before touchdown. When I beheld the surprised judgment on both faces, I decided to listen with greater attention to discern what candy-related gaffe I committed.

The flight from Phoenix back to Minneapolis started out pleasantly enough. I sat in the aisle seat and the woman in the middle seat gushed her eagerness to watch her son play his first college football for St. Cloud the next day, earning her the plane name, Football Mom. I liked her immediately. Before takeoff, she announced her intention to sleep during the flight, which made me enjoy her even more. I found myself more gregarious, knowing I wouldn't have to sustain conversation the entire time.

The guy at the window leaned into our conversation, wanting inclusion, and a few times here and there, he contributed a "yup." He wore a country-style shirt unbuttoned enough to see chest hair, which earned him the plane name, Urban Cowboy.

The plane took off.

She slept.

Urban Cowboy stared out the window.

I read.

Toward the end of the flight she awoke and brought her seat forward. About that time I smelled something suspicious. Marijuana. I smelled it *strong*. Could someone truly dare to smoke weed on a packed-to-capacity airplane? Couldn't you get arrested for that? I wondered if the air marshal would make a dramatic bust in front of all of us. I would like to see that.

I sniffed the air.

Football Mom watched me wrinkle my nose a few times and sniff like a bloodhound before asking, "What? What's going on?"

I said, "Nothing. I thought I smelled something."

I went back to reading.

She needled me, saying, "What did you think you smelled? Do you still smell it?"

The marijuana aroma wafted over me again so I said, "*There*! Can you smell that? Doesn't it smell like someone is smoking pot?"

She inhaled deeply as if the flight attendant had delivered scrumptious butternut squash soup to her fold-down tray, which caught the attention of Urban Cowboy. He asked, "What's going on? What are you guys doing?"

Football Mom leaned over conspiratorially and said, "The Aisle Guy smells marijuana."

I guess we all received plane names.

Urban Cowboy joined our sniffing contest and honestly, the three of us huffing stale airplane air looked mighty suspicious. I'm surprised the people in Row 35 didn't turn around to yell at us to knock it the hell off.

Urban Cowboy asked, "Where'd he smell it? From the front?"

I was no longer confident what I smelled, a whiff of something long gone at this point, so I downplayed my experience.

Football Mom asked, "Do you *know* what pot smells like?"

I hesitated. When someone asks me about my familiarity with recreational drugs, I try to avoid answering that question directly and say something vague like, "I went to college in the 80s" and leave it at that. I never tripped acid or did anything harder, but I may want to run for Senate someday and I'd like to keep my deniability options open.

I did live in San Francisco for four months and whether you smoked pot or not, merely existing in that city becomes a crash course in all things related to marijuana: the surprising public places you can get away with smoking and household items you can turn into bongs. I once witnessed a Diet Pepsi can transformed into an effective delivery mechanism with only seven punctures. San Franciscans' ingenuity amazed me. Several times while visiting new California friends they asked, "Can I offer you a glass of water or perhaps a joint?"

Yeah, I know how pot smells. (Also, I went to college in the 80s.)

Football Mom hailed from California (by way of connecting flight in Phoenix) and confessed she too would recognize marijuana's distinct odor, although she didn't smell it right then. Urban Cowboy chimed in with, "Hells yeah, I'd know it," and he did not shy from this conversational direction. The two of them began discussing where to find pot, which turned into how to grow pot, and the maximum quantity of pot you could grow without police detection.

I lost interest.

I wanted to finish my book.

They kept chatting, including me occasionally. I would glance up and nod or say, "Yeah, sounds about right," and go back to reading. This turned out to be a mistake on my part.

When the captain announced our imminent landing, I pulled out spearmint gum from my camo pants' side pocket and offered them both something chewable to pop their ears on the way down. They each took a piece and thanked me.

Football Mom dug around in her purse and offered us each a hard candy. She said, "It's homemade. My friend made it."

I liked this, this 30,000-foot gift exchange. We'll never see each other again. We never exchanged real names. Yet we gave each other tokens to say, "I enjoyed this time with you."

The butterscotch-colored candy had been shaped into a heart. Cute. I unwrapped it and popped it into my mouth.

Then, the shocked looks from Football Mom and Urban Cowboy.

Sensing my faux pas, I listened to their ongoing conversation with renewed interest.

They still chatted about marijuana. Almost fifteen or twenty minutes passed since our Row 36 sniffing contest, and I had tuned out most of it. But they were *still* eagerly discussing the topic and Football Mom was showing off her California medicinal purpose card and discussing her favorite brands.

Uh oh.

Like an idiot, I realized what I had smelled earlier was *her*. When she woke, she had moved her seat upright and the resulting stir of air wafted the marijuana clinging to her clothes toward me. That had to be it.

The candy dissolved on my tongue quickly. It was sweet. Tangy. Almost a hint of herb.

I interrupted their quiet, intense conversation to ask in a hushed tone, "Excuse me, but was this candy laced with marijuana?"

(Who even says, "laced with marijuana?" That's language from a 1950s film strip meant to scare sixth-graders.)

Football Mom looked at me with big eyes. "Yes. It was."

"Oh." I didn't know what else to say. The candy had already dissolved on my tongue.

We all stayed quiet for a moment.

I asked, "Am I about to get really high?"

With equal solemnity, she said, "Yes. You are."

I nodded and faced the front. Another fifteen minutes or so remained before touchdown. Soon I would be completely, balls-out stoned in a flying metal box full of people.

Not. Good.

I turned to her. "I guess you're not the air marshal on this flight, huh?"

With a smirk, she said, "I guess you're not either."

On the plus side, I now understood why Football Mom and Urban Cowboy's eyes had opened wide. When she gave me her special candy, she had no expectation I would instantly pop it into my mouth. Who knows—she may have even said, "Don't eat this until you're at home," or implied a veiled warning a few minutes earlier to which I absently replied, "Yeah, sounds about right." I probably should have listened with greater attention to the conversation.

But who gives pot candy to a stranger on an airplane? Hell, who *brings* pot candy on an airplane? I didn't even know you could, I dunno, *candy it up*. I assumed you could only bake it into cookies and brownies. Shows you what I know.

Like guilty teenagers, Urban Cowboy and Football Mom ditched me as soon as we disembarked, and they were probably smart to do so. I was already acting weird. I walked by every TSA agent talking to myself, saying, "Stay cool. Stay cool. Don't do anything stupid." For me, these thoughts are generally the precursor to my doing something unbelievably stupid. I don't need marijuana to make myself conspicuous or suspicious. I manage quite well on my own, thank you.

I ordered my skin not to sweat and then got angry with myself for disobeying.

I held my shit together until baggage claim, when I started giggling. I mean, c'mon. All those identical black bags spinning around the silver, serpentine circle like burned hot dogs under a shitty gas station's rotating heat lamps. Everyone stared at the show with exhausted eyes, blearily watching those same hot dogs spin around and around, as if reluctant to pick a bloated pig's intestine, pour ketchup on it, and go home.... It was all so ridiculous. Then I got the munchies.

Yup. Baked.

So I started laughing.

Took a cab home and managed to give my cab driver the right address. I stayed respectably quiet, admiring the trees and pretty, pretty lights flashing by.

So pretty. So very pretty.

I imagine there are several morals you can draw from this tale, including the obvious, *don't take candy from strangers*, an adage usually reserved for 10-year-olds and not middle-aged men. Meh. Too obvious. Perhaps one might say, "Listen to the conversations you're involved in," and that's a good one, I guess.

I'm the kind of man who makes a lot of mistakes. Sometimes they work out and you get to appreciate the pretty, sparkling lights from the back of a cab. Sometimes those mistakes end in disaster. It's hard to know if it's a mistake when you're giggling about the results.

I think my take-away here is to always bring breath mints to baggage claim because you never know when you're going to feel the overwhelming urge to hug strangers and say, "Is it me or does the luggage carousel look a silver snake carrying rotating sausages?"

THE BEST NEW YORK SANDWICH

WHEN I announced my intention to live in New York City for a month researching a book, a number of friends advocated for restaurants and culinary experiences I simply had to try. I heard things like, "They have the *best* pizza," or "Nobody knows about this place, but their curries are to die for." Best ramen noodles, best cheesecakes, and best donuts. Best brunch. Best street food.

The best gay ice cream.

It's not surprising.

We all want to own a little piece of this American mecca, to know a secret spot for perfect cranberry muffins or cherry crepes. To know a *best* food item is to know New York in a way others do not, which means somehow New York knows you love her, so she let you find the best pierogi outside Poland.

I'm no different.

I wanted to have my own unique New York experience, to discover and love this city in a way others do not normally see. To find something utterly exceptional and yet somehow perfectly representative of New York. And while I could have sought out the best New York pastrami, I wanted to understand more about the hundreds of homeless people I had passed in my few short weeks in the Big Apple. I decided to be homeless for a day.

I woke at 6 a.m. in my Chelsea studio apartment, my headquarters for May, and dressed like I often do: camo pants, gray shirt, flannel jacket. Having lived in New York for the previous two weeks, I had discovered my wardrobe already mimicked homeless attire, so I didn't require any costuming. I hadn't shaved in a few days, so I was all kinds of scruffy and that morning I resisted showering, on principle alone. My cardboard sign said, "ANYTHING HELPS," and I drew sad little dollar signs at the bottom, a suggestion for those who didn't understand my words.

I hopped the downtown 2 train to Brooklyn and by 7 a.m. got off at Wall Street. I wanted to be ready for morning rush hour. On the subway, I contemplated why *this* experience, why impersonate a homeless person? There's a certain offensiveness in pretending to be homeless, as if spending a few hours sitting on concrete is enough to understand. Plenty of hipster reporters had already done "what it's like" journalistic essays about the homeless experience and after spending a week in ratty jeans, they returned to Chelsea brunches and weekends at the Met. Living two weeks in New York with no friends or family, very little connection to others while passing hundreds and thousands of people in the street, I had to admit that even with a roof over my head, I felt a little displaced and homeless. I slept on a mattress on the floor, with a card table and one chair my only furniture. I wanted my outsides to match my insides, if only for a little while. This is part of New York's story—feeling lonely and forgotten.

My first location wasn't great. After a half hour I moved to sit right *on* Wall Street, near the subway entrance, down the street from the famous diamond emporium, Tiffany & Co. Across the street, a colossal granite fortress (which I assumed to be a grand, luxury hotel) presented stout Greek columns and a tuxedoed doorman wearing a tall top hat. Every once in a while the tuxedoed man would catch my eye and sternly communicate, *Don't come over here.* I would glare back, *I will if I feel like it.*

I had grabbed a Starbucks cup from the trash and wiped it dry. Placed it before me with my sign and waited.

People walked by.

I contemplated the best way to conduct myself. I kept my hands free from my pocket, fingers interlaced in front of me. I figured that made me appear harmless. Vulnerable.

I sat.

I studied every cigarette butt in a 30-foot radius, every gum stain now a circular black tattoo on the city sidewalk.

I watched a clutch of moms bundle their kids into a school bus. I didn't realize New York kids got bussed to school. Huh. Interesting. I watched with curiosity and realized one mother deliberately stood between me and her kids, because, oh right. I was a panhandler.

New Yorkers on their way to work clipped by. Cell phone chatter. People with coffee. For a while, nobody gave me money. I worried that somehow I was doing it wrong. Maybe it just wasn't busy enough yet.

When the first guy dropped money in my cup, I was stunned. I kept forgetting why I was here. He gave me $2.50 in quarters. He also gave me this big grin, as if he felt delight to see me. Then, he darted to the curb and into a cab. Almost immediately after that, an older man with silver hair dropped a dollar in my cup. He smiled big, too.

I hadn't expected the smiling. I don't know why.

A young guy, construction worker, whom I heard speaking Spanish on his phone a moment earlier, dropped a dollar in my cup and showered me with this dazzling, unrestrained smile. It felt like a second-date smile, the kind you get from someone who is happy to see you again and he wants you to know it. I don't know why I was shocked but I was. He moved four feet away and started a new phone conversation, obviously in no hurry to get away from me.

A brown-haired woman veered off her linear path to pass me a dollar. She handed it to me with great seriousness and turned to walk away. She was the first who didn't smile. I wondered about her life and the kindness in her demanding she stray from her trajectory. As she crossed the street, she looked over her shoulder at me and smiled big. She waved, as if leaving a friend after a coffee date. Ah, *there* was the smile.

Wall street came to life as the day began in earnest. As more and more New Yorkers passed my way, the frequency of donations increased.

A black woman in her 40s gave me money and said, "God bless." A Korean man in a pink shirt and white knit vest handed me a dollar and smiled shyly. He bolted away—late for something it seemed—but he made time to stop for me. A woman with the most complicated bun and tri-shaded maroon hair gave me money and murmured something like, "Mmmhmm," before disappearing into the flow.

Black people. White people. Older. Young people. Casual dress. Suits. Everyone who contributed looked at me, looked me in the eye for a brief second.

A handsome young buck, filling out an expensive burgundy shirt and silk tie handed me a dollar. He sported reflective sunglasses and like many others, had ear buds jammed in his skull. His hair was freshly shorn, stylish, very Abercrombie & Fitch. I assumed I would see a smirk or a wrinkled judgment cross his face as he handed me the dollar. Something like, *Jesus, what happened to you, man?*

Nope.

His mouth formed a terse line, like he understood the seriousness of my situation. He nodded at me. Respectfully. And then he was lost in the crowd.

Mostly everyone ignored me, walking by on their way to busy lives. I didn't resent them. I'd walk right by me, too. Hell, I had walked by the homeless some days, not even seeing them, other days giving money. Who knows why I did either? But on *my* homeless day, I wondered about people and if they had donated money on the previous block or the previous day, the way other people generously donated to me today.

I took the subway to Times Square for a different audience and experienced the same kindnesses, people who looked me in the eye and smiled. Nodded. A woman gave me two crumpled dollars and boarded her bus. An older man, possibly Japanese, stopped and pulled out his wallet. He made time.

A twelve-year-old kid raced close to me, dropped a dollar in my cup, and darted away, like a sparrow. I bet he was a tourist and asked his parents' permission to do this random act of kindness. A toddler waddled by and seeing me at her eye-level, she burst into giggles. I waved and she screeched with delight, looking back as her mom led them toward the theaters.

A guy with frazzled hair, donning ear buds and dangling a cigarette from his lower lip, approached and put two bucks in my cup. He stared into my eyes. Without words he somehow communicated, *I understand*. I tried to fathom what he meant by that look, what he had gone through, his life experiences, but the only message I received was him letting me know, *I understand*.

I cried when he walked away because he expressed such earnestness and seemed genuinely worried about me. Turns out, the compassion and friendliness I had not witnessed in my fellow New Yorkers for the past two weeks was everywhere around me. I decided they save it, however, for those who genuinely need it.

After the experiment was over, I gave away all the money I collected to my fellow panhandlers, those who weren't experimenting with homelessness, but forced to live it, day after day. As I handed them money, I made sure to look each person in the eye and smile big. I now know how much that matters in a city of millions, that millisecond connection suggesting, *I see you*.

While at my Wall Street location, an Asian-American woman handed me an aluminum foil-wrapped square. After I watched her stride away, I observed she carried a brown bag for her lunch. I unwrapped the tin foil to find her homemade sandwich.

She made it with processed cheese, the cheap kind that remains imprinted with its individual plastic wrap. The meat was thinly sliced, a hybrid of ham and pastrami, one of those sandwich meats rather difficult to name. Ambiguous flavor. Wheat bread. Mayonnaise. It wasn't fully cut in half. The bottom bread was barely perforated. A half-assed job done by someone in a hurry. I know. I've made sandwiches like that.

Obviously, she made it for herself, but when she encountered someone who she felt needed it more, she did not hesitate. She gifted it to me and disappeared into the crowd of busy professionals.

The gift of her sandwich was too personal, too intimate. I could not toss it and it felt wrong to pass it to someone else. So I consumed her sandwich slowly while sitting on a bench before the impressive Wall Street Exchange. Swear to God, it was the best sandwich you will ever find in New York.

SECRET VODKA PARTY

LIKE MILLIONS of other kids in high school, I wasn't invited to the cool kid parties. Or, *any* party. Four years missing high school party invitations culminated in the biggest snub during our senior class trip. While visiting a remote resort in Wisconsin, the entire senior class ditched me and two others while they partied—the big blowout bash—in the woods. In a class of thirty-six (yes, you read that correctly: thirty and then six), the omission of three was duly noted.

I felt hurt but couldn't blame them. My dad taught English at our high school. You can't party with a teacher's straight-laced kid.

Let's face it. Everyone's got a boo-hoo story about high school rejection, feeling left out. Who knows how many of our stories are valid and reflect reality? Regardless, the painful feelings of separation and isolation were real.

Very real.

These surprisingly vigorous feelings made me apprehensive about attending my first Gay Romance Literature writers' conference. I felt excitement but also dread, like the first day of high school. I knew a handful of writers and readers from emails and Facebook posts, but how would we manage in person when we couldn't type LOL? Online pals don't always translate into real-world friends.

Thinking of the upcoming GayRomLit conference, I could easily project uncomfortable parallels to high school. What if I showed up and nobody wanted to talk to me? Would I eat alone in the cafeteria pretending it was exactly what I wanted? Would I once again miss out on all the cool kids' parties?

After all, I'd only written *one* book. Other attending writers had published dozens. They had more readers, more writing skills, more marketing skills, more everything. I struggle to not feel insecure around talented people.

Nevertheless, I decided to enjoy myself and be ridiculously me, despite the teenage drama in my head. If I didn't fit in, so be it. In high school, I had comforted myself by arguing they never saw the *real* me. I hadn't revealed my whole self so their rejection couldn't hurt. It did hurt, but I tried to comfort myself with this thinking. These days, if I am to be rejected, I would prefer the reason be I shared my glorious, idiot self.

After preparing for so much rejection, imagine my freshman writer surprise to feel wildly embraced beyond all reasonable expectations. While trying to check in at the host hotel, I ran into twelve or thirteen people I "knew" online. We hugged, chatted, hugged, chatted, and they introduced me to their friends, some of whom said, "Oh sure, I've heard of you."

It took me 45 minutes to check in and get my luggage upstairs. A new friend, Anne, followed me upstairs and we chattered non-stop as I unpacked. She extracted some awful clothes from my duffel bag and held a shirt aloft, saying, "I can't believe you packed *this*."

I loved her instantly.

All weekend, instead of waiting to belong, I witnessed writers and readers *creating* belonging. Come join us. Who are you? Sit at our table. What do you write? Who do you read?

The first conference night, despite feeling overwhelmed and shy, I joined an impromptu lobby party where I experienced, for the first time, cake-flavored vodka. These new friends showered me with eager questions and before long, we traded anecdotes and lewd flirts as if this night was our fourth successful date, the one where we have sex.

Hoping to return the favor later that weekend (and feeling a smidge guilty for gulping the last of the cake vodka), I purchased several bottles of cake vodka. Carmel-flavored vodka, too. Friday night, I boldly invited new friends to meet me in the lobby for a drink around 10 p.m. Nothing formal. No guest list. Just show up and pass the word.

A dozen people appeared at the appointed hour. Then, more. As the lobby grew crowded, we found an unlocked hotel ballroom to create our impromptu bar. We swilled vodka shots from plastic cups, everyone saying, "Wow, this tastes exactly like cake." We marveled at how vodka scientists bonded cake molecules with liquor and wondered what could happen if these bright minds tried to solve something like, you know, cancer.

New conference friends passing through the hotel hallway followed our laughter and poked their heads in the open door. Can we come in?

Yes. Stay. Bring your whole self.

In a quiet corner, I chatted with someone who felt challenged by this much extroversion. I confessed my own similar fears. We toasted with caramel vodka. I met two people I secretly admired, celebs in the GayRomLit world who happened to wander in and opted to stay. I provided detailed cunnilingus lessons on a chocolate vagina pop purchased earlier in the day from an X-rated candy store and I'm chagrined to recall someone in the room filmed it with their smart phone. I probably shouldn't have done that.

When I chomped off the top, women in the room screamed in empathetic agony.

Erica from Iceland approached me and shyly inquired if she might go to her room and return with several bottles of her country's liquor. She had been hoping for an impromptu party just like this one. A few moments later she returned with a bottle of Brennivin and Opal, two mysterious Icelandic treats.

I could write paragraphs about each new friend at the secret vodka party and how they blasted their unique flavor of love, but Erica deserves a shout-out. Before the conference, she noted her local GLBT youth center lacked any current fiction, nothing new on the shelves for many years. Budgets for gay fiction do not exist. She asked GayRomLit authors to donate a hard copy, if at all possible, and she would carry them back to Iceland.

Seventy authors cheerfully agreed. *Seventy*!

Erica paid for the shipping.

I felt proud and grateful to co-host with her.

Her Opal liquor became a huge success because it tasted so awful.

Everyone who partook immediately grimaced at the taste of bitter, hard licorice and some unnamable flavor akin to burned wheat toast. After the initial licorice subsided and the drinker's involuntary reaction of gasping, "Oh God," that same taster inevitably smacked his or her lips together a few more times, experiencing a more pleasant sensation and would then would say, "That was terrible. Pour me another shot."

Erica laughed freely, glad to talk about Iceland and the many uses for this strange liquor.

More people arrived and we welcomed them eagerly, found them chairs and poured them shots. We laughed about books, sex, writing habits, and people we admired sitting two chairs away. As more found their way to us, I said to my friend Anne, "How does everyone know we're here?"

"Oh sorry," she said cheerfully. "I tweeted you were hosting a secret vodka party. Told everyone to come to this ballroom."

She smiled and resumed crocheting a blue penis. "I mentioned your oral skills on the chocolate vagina."

About this time, one conference organizer pulled me out into the hallway to stare me in the eye and say, "This is *your* party. You're responsible for this room. *You*. Clean up when it's over." While she is a powerful and imposing woman, I did not feel intimidated. No, her message was not a threat, but instead communicated, *I trust you. I believe in you. Make this right.* In that moment, I realized I could check something off my bucket list: host a high school party.

I can't say I've spent much time fretting over high school parties I never attended. I had friends in high school and I now understand they saw more of my true self than I imagined. Still, once in a while I feel I missed an important high school tradition, a piece of American life passed me by.

As I returned to our party room, several faces turned my way to make sure things were okay. I nodded. All was well. Although not everyone I had come to love at the conference attended the Secret Vodka Party, I felt warm to experience so much rich, loving acceptance in one room. Strangers and friends laughing, drinking, sharing vulnerable stories, sharing their true selves.

In the corner, Anne smiled and crocheted a penis.

I heard someone gag on Erica's Opal liquor and say, "Ugh. *Awful.* Pour me one more."

ADVENTURE DAY MAGIC!

I KNOW how you're supposed to celebrate birthdays: cake, candles, joyful dinner with loving friends, making out with your significant other, champagne. Cards with jokes about getting old. I've spent birthdays that way and loved the crap out of each one. You never have to talk me into cake. Just hand over a fork.

But.

I also dig spending my birthday alone.

That's kind of messed up, I suppose. What kind of anti-social creep likes to dine alone on his birthday? Who turns off the phone and reads a book by a stream instead of raking in the calls and texts, affectionate jeers, that once-a-year chorus of HAPPY BIRTHDAY! I will admit on my birthday morning to waiting by the phone for my mom and dad to call and sing me happy birthday. I love that tradition, even more so after losing Dad.

Mom called this morning and she sang. Her voice was beautiful.

After parental singing is achieved, I often spend my birthday similar to how I approach New Year's Eve: alone, reflecting on where I've been and where I'm headed. But maybe with a bit of adventure thrown in.

On my last birthday, I bought a gorilla suit and went banana shopping at a major grocery store. I hugged the store manager who posed for photographs. With a friend's assistance, we harassed my best pals, Dave and Don. After dark, I monkeyed up to their living room windows, tapping and doodling my giant gorilla fingers on the glass until one of them caught my ape face outside and screamed obscenities unfit for human consumption (and this is coming from me, who believes the word *fucking* makes a handy adjective).

As might be expected, they chased me through their yard. I threw bananas at them and then escaped into my friend's waiting Ford Taurus. Dave chased the getaway car down the alley, hurling a banana at our retreat. The gorilla returned ten minutes later for another sneak attack.

I love my birthday.

Well, today's birthday got a little out of hand.

My driver's license expired today, requiring a trip to the DMV for renewal. I tend to regard my necessary trips to DMV not as an administrative chore, but an opportunity for performance art. I take theme photos for my driver's license. I did *giddy* one year wearing a bow tie and an unnatural grin which made all those who observed my driver's license uncomfortable. I've done *furious* and *surprised*.

One of my favorites was *fear*. When the DMV employee in a lackluster voice said, "Smile," I arranged my face into an about-to-be-murdered expression. She looked at the resulting photograph and frowned. She said, "Let's try this again. And this time, *big* smile." I nodded vehemently, because who doesn't want to appear their best on their driver's license? I rewarded her with another please-don't-kill-me expression and when she confirmed the second try, she grimly said, "Good," and gave up. Some people just don't know how to smile.

This year's theme: *Magic!*

Of course, this required I dye my hair black, since all powerful magicians have jet black hair. Everyone knows this. Sure, Roy (of Siegfried and Roy) was a blond magician but he was attacked by a tiger. Even tigers know magicians must be raven-haired. I am so very blond people tell me blond jokes and then apologize. To pass as a magician, I required matching black eyebrows I could arch meaningfully to indicate *I have secrets*. And, of course, a matching black goatee. I would wear an expression suggesting power and intrigue and forces of nature answering to my command. I would create...

Magic!

I called Ann, my best friend of twenty-five years, to inform her of my birthday *Magic!* strategy. Her official response was, "Oh no. Oh no, oh no, oh no..."

I couldn't uncover a single flaw in my plan but Ann dug up a few: they could arrest me, everyone will know it's not my real color, I've never dyed my own hair, *ever*, so I have no clue what I'm doing, my Goth hair would represent me on my license for the next four years, etc. Even if she suspects her advice will fall on deaf ears because I'm determined to be an idiot, Ann feels obliged to remind me when there could be consequences requiring bail money. For a college professor in gifted education, she gives surprisingly good legal advice.

"It'll be great," I assured her. "You'll see."

Skipping ahead, let me just say this. Things didn't go great.

Brimming with unflappable and unjustified confidence, I headed to the local pharmacy and proudly asked for their hair dye products. I returned a minute later to ask where to find the *men's* hair dye products. I returned a minute later to ask where to find hair dye you can wash out an hour later after the joke's over.

Armed with my spray-on dye, I proudly scurried home.

Like a true professional, I used blue painter's tape to cordon off my forehead and sides of my face. I snapped a selfie of my taped head to send to Ann when she's having a very bad day. After completing the spray job, I removed the wonderful blue tape to reveal a clean, even horizon right at my hairline. I gingerly massaged it with a towel to blend in the crisp line, making it look more natural.

I texted photos to Ann who called immediately to laugh so hard in my ear that she failed to create sound. I worried she might die and when I inquired after her health, she merely whispered, *"Air."*

Since I had a hair dye expert on the phone, I expressed my worry about the uneven black stripes cutting swatches across the back of my head. From what I could see in the mirror I held back there, I looked like a sick tiger. I asked, "What if someone at the DMV figures it out?"

Ann laughed even harder. In a barely audible voice (which I'm confident was accompanied by her wiping away tears), she said, "Oh honey, nobody—*nobody*—will care about your little prank. Their focus will be on feeling humiliation for your awful dye job."

We agreed I needed to bring a clean towel, the spray-on dye, and the toothbrush I used to create eyebrows on my face. (My eyebrows are so blond I have caught people unabashedly staring at me trying to determine if they exist.) Against Ann's sage advice, I decided to wear a baseball cap to cover up my striped tiger skull. I promised not to let it touch the front.

She tried to warn me. "No, no. No hat. That's not going to work out well. Big mistake."

Kudos, Ann. She would eventually be proven right again. Sometimes Ann is like the Greek character of legend, Cassandra of Troy, a doom-and-gloom prophetess cursed to always predict an accurate future to disbelievers.

I blasted the air conditioning all the way to the DMV so nothing would melt on my head. I had discovered an unfortunate side effect of low-quality spray-on hair dye: it drips down your head in August heat. I arrived at the DMV more or less intact, no new black streaks dripping down my face. I coolly took the number sixteen from the red dispenser.

I was cool. Very cool.

Just another raven-haired man (possibly a magician) come to renew his driver's license. Nothing to see here, folks, except possibly a dove flying free from my sleeve.

Someone behind the counter called out, "Ninety three."

Ninety three?

Fuck. Sixteen wasn't even in the same decade.

I had assumed this errand of deception would end quickly. I had been hoping for a get-in and get-out caper. Realistically, who assumes that? *I'll quickly pop on over to the DMV.* Who thinks that? Nobody. You bring a book, a deck of cards, and maybe a pack of cigs to trade for food.

I texted my plight to Ann. This could take a while. What if my hair melted before an audience? There were not enough emoticons and variations of LOL invented to contain her mirth.

I lowered myself with resignation between two individuals who were pleasant enough when I first sat down. I am sad to report my neighborly relationships soon soured.

Another unfortunate decision I made was to compensate for the obnoxious stench associated with cheap, spray-on hair dye with an abusive quantity of patchouli oil, the closest thing I own to cologne. Actually, the slippery liquid boasts an explosive mixture of sandalwood, patchouli and other woodsy oils combined in an empty poppers bottle, a flirty gift from a sexy pagan man I knew years ago. On nights when I wander through my neighborhood pretending I'm hiking a redwood forest, I dab two or three drops on my moustache to facilitate my imagination. Two or three drops is plenty. On this *Magic!* birthday, I slathered my entire face. In short, I reeked, a cross between burnt-ozone hair dye and an angry forest.

One of my neighbors in the plastic scoop chair next to mine got up and walked away. He preferred to stand for the next few hours rather than sit next to my over-chemicalized skull. My other neighbor was content to stay and shoot me dirty glances. When I texted Ann the latest issue, my overwhelming stench, she replied, "This keeps getting better and better."

My only hope was the lines would move quickly. Yet every person's appeal to the DMV employees took fifteen minutes. How could every single person's issue have such complications? I could overhear number Ninety Eight at the counter, a middle-aged chatter bug who, upon gaining access to a real-live DMV employee, used the opportunity to expand upon the topic of cars he once loved. After ten minutes I almost walked over to him and said, "Ninety Eight, nobody cares about your neighbor's Jeep and how much he sold it for online. Fill out your damn forms. My hair's melting."

If I had been my blond self, I would have done it. I'm a blond. Who cares if I'm an idiot? But as a raven-haired man, I owed a responsibility to my new people to keep it cool.

Chill.

Magic!

Much, much later, possibly years later, the gruff lady working the middle counter barked out, "Six!"

She embraced the DMV stereotype. Her hair was gray and matted in a way suggesting she did nothing more than go home, sleep, and come back to work. She wore pincher eyeglasses slung low so she could fix an angry stare over the top. If Ninety Eight had been her customer, she wouldn't have tolerated any of his bullshit about the neighbor's Jeep.

I texted Ann I had to go dark. Although my number, sixteen, was still ten digits away, I needed to calculate the odds of her being the one to call my number. Plus, I wanted to work through my answers to awkward questions about my hair care. What if someone decided to challenge me? Ann begged me to text her from jail.

In the meantime, nobody approached for six.

"Seven," she called out. "Seven!"

Nobody came.

"Eight!" she yelled.

"*Nine!*"

"Ten!" she said, followed immediately by angrily exclamation. "*You're kidding me.*"

I'd watched more than a few people reach their personal breaking point, stand, crumple their number, and storm out, huffing. I wasn't the only one who'd had no clue how many hours could be spent at the DMV.

In an accusatory voice, she yelled, "*Eleven.*"

Nobody came forth.

"Twelve!"

She grew righteously pissed at those of us remaining as she continued to belch out numbers. "*My God. Thirteen!*"

If, gentle reader, you have already skipped to the conclusion nobody would step out between thirteen and my number sixteen, you are correct.

By the time she bellowed "*Sixteen*," she had worked herself into a frothy rage and she despised all of us dopes staring at her, slack-jawed losers, cowards who refused to step forward.

Given my unusual circumstances, I had hoped to avoid this flavor of DMV rage. I wanted to text Ann and beg her to help me, but given how I ignored all her other sound advice, even I couldn't see how asking her help in dealing with the furious DMV employee would do any good.

I walked slowly to the angry woman's station.

As I arrived, her much younger coworker leaned over and said to my lady, "Everybody's mad at me today."

The coworker was no powerful black-haired like me and George Clooney and Demi Moore. And Cher (sometimes). She wore short brown hair and an expression of sadness. Clearly she had not worked at the DMV long enough to transform the hurt into hate.

In her gruff tone, my lady said, "You get used to it."

I felt sad.

They have hard jobs. People yell at them about their fees, their hours, the complication of forms. All problems they did not create. All problems they cannot solve. Earlier I witnessed a man argue with an employee about handing over his motorcycle's deed. She kept repeating politely, "It's the *law*, sir. I have to collect it." I remembered the DMV employee who gave me two chances to correct my smile when creating my *fear* driver's license photo. She had tried to help me. Her humanity shone through.

I turned toward the woman who expressed sadness and said, "I'm mad at you and I'm not even in your line. But I'm *furious*!"

She looked at me in shock and I suddenly remembered my plan to not draw undo attention to myself. What happened to playing it cool, dark-haired man? Even while pretending to be someone different, I am still me, saying stupid things, ignoring good advice.

"I'm furious," I said and raised my fists in the air, shaking them like an angry Hulk. "I could scream."

She laughed, my angry lady laughed, and I laughed too. My dad said shit like that all the time to strangers and it worked.

We giggled more and I said, "I'm sorry people are douche bags to you today. That must be hard."

She laughed and thanked me, and my lady, the one who had practically screamed out the number sixteen, said to me with good cheer, "C'mon. Vision test."

Then, the big moment: the photo.

I took off the ball cap. Sat on the stool.

She said, "Smile."

I said, "I don't have a great smile, so if you don't mind, I won't."

She shrugged.

I had perfected my magician look in the bathroom mirror—one eyebrow raised suggestively, my lips curled into a mysterious, all-knowing smirk, my shimmering black hair....

She positioned herself behind the camera and I adopted my *Magic!* face.

I saw a tiny click motion from the camera and being very eager to leave, I leaned forward to stand up, eyes wide open and two inches away from the monstrous flash as it illuminated, burning out my retinas.

"We have to retake it," she said. "That little click means the flash is about to go off."

No shit.

Normally when staring at a camera flash, you see a purple spot before your eyes, but this time there was nothing *but* an enormous purple spot filling my entire line of vision. I couldn't have found the front door if the building were on fire. I had stared right into the flash as it blazed.

After the second photo, she said to me, "We have to retake that one too. You've got a big black smudge on your forehead. You can clean up in the mirror to your left."

She handed me a couple paper towels and I turned to their tiny mirror. I panicked. I couldn't see anything but purple shapes. I waited and waited (and she waited for me) until finally I could see a fat black line of melted hair dye creating a crescent moon on my forehead. Almost like a person wearing a baseball cap might get if he accidentally forgot and rubbed the cap against his forehead.

I wiped frantically, but the smudge kept smearing. I couldn't see very well—that flash was still burning my eyes. Then, the paper towels touched the side of my coal-colored hair, and black chalk wafted onto my face. I scrubbed a few more times, aware this took much longer than it should and she was undoubtedly staring.

I mumbled out the words, "I worked on my car today."

What the hell? *Why the hell did I say that*?

I'm sure she rolled her eyes, but I couldn't actually see her.

I spit on my fingers to create moisture to rub my blackening face, but I discovered the patchouli oil I'd applied lavishly bonded to the black flakes, and furious rubbing only worked it in deeper, making my skin tone an unhealthy gray ash.

When I finished scrubbing my face and dared to glance in the mirror, I now saw (behind my purple spots) a terrified coal miner. Who the hell was that man staring back at me in sheer panic? A grifter? Ex-con? Bounty hunter? I certainly was not *Magic!* but who ever is? We're all a big surprise, even to ourselves, even on our birthday.

She snapped the photo and said nothing. I think maybe she was pretty cool after all.

The DMV will mail me my new driver's license in seven to ten days. In the meantime, I will feel like a kid again, excitedly checking the mail, eager to find a wonderful birthday surprise.

That's the best part of my birthday, feeling young, feeling goofy. Getting excited about being me, whether dark-haired or blond.

Well, that and birthday cake.

SETTING THE RECORD STRAIGHT

LAST WEEK, a certain author who I will not name (Jenna Blum) wrote a blog entry in which certain other unnamed persons (me) were accused of being found in bed with a female blow-up doll aptly named Plastiqua. Ms. Blum offered photographic evidence.

Me.

In bed.

Naked.

With the blow-up doll.

Like many modern political candidates who suffer a slight shadow on their otherwise sterling reputations, I desire to clear my name and set the record straight. Like those same political candidates, I'm not going to do so because the events are mostly true. Instead, I'm going to get all huffy and act indignant as if you have a lot of nerve looking right at the actual truth.

Finally, I'm going to try to distract you from the real issues (why does a grown man have so many stories about a blow-up doll?) by focusing on *my* version of the truth, a story that must be told. And by *must*, I mean nobody wants to hear this but I want to tell it.

Plastiqua.

Yes, Senators. I knew her.

Yes, yes, the other part is true, we were naked in bed together, but I can explain. *Hear me out*, Senators. Hear me out.

(I enjoy picturing my life explained before a senate sub-committee.)

When I moved into my first Minneapolis apartment on Emerson Avenue, Jenna lived upstairs and clomped around the hardwood floors in her equestrian boots, causing me to wonder if some days she had forgotten to leave the horse at the stables. Clompity, clomp, clomp.

She will deny it and even swears she wasn't out riding horses, but this is my senate hearing, so let's say she also wore one of those funny, black riding hats and a cardinal-red jacket, her bouncy, blond hair curling down her back.

Having bonded over our mutual love for deviled eggs, we became friendly acquaintances. When we discovered we both loved writing fiction, we became drinking buddies. Over gold vinyl wallpaper and greasy burgers at Matt's Bar and Grill, our twisted friendship was cemented. She introduced me to Plastiqua, the blow-up doll in question. Senators, Plastiqua was not my property. Not at first.

Plastiqua never said much, given her mouth was stenciled, her lips factory-drawn. She didn't have any functioning lady parts, let's get those details out in the open. Well, other than inflatable boobs. No, throughout her naked career, she remained an asexual bachelor party prop and nothing more. Although it seems rather cruel to make a blow-up doll with no sexual parts. I mean, what's the point?

Jenna and I initiated friendships with the other apartment building dwellers, mostly as insurance in case any of us went missing, presumably at the hands of the creepy on-site manager who got stoned in the basement where he practiced taxidermy on bats. We friended the idealistic lawyer across the hall and the sweet, young eco-political couple in the apartment next to his, confident any one of those three were destined for a senate seat in your august house, sirs and madams. Occasionally the mysterious music girl down the hall joined us, but she attended a lot of concerts, so we didn't see her as often. Every time we assumed she had been taxidermied in the creepy basement, she surprised one of us by checking her mail in the foyer.

During group dinners, Plastiqua joined us at the table. We dragged her to the couch for movie nights. Often, one of us would dry hump her to make the others laugh, after which Jenna played the jealous girlfriend and beat Plastiqua fiercely for being a slut. Unless Jenna dry humped Plastiqua first.

Esteemed Senators, Plastiqua had earned her place as a comrade.

One wintery Saturday afternoon, the apartment friends in question planned a late-night sledding outing after everyone's Saturday evening plans concluded. But then it got cold. Then colder. Crazy cold. When I realized the temperature had dropped to 15 degrees below zero, I decided our sledding plans would be null and void, so I didn't bother heading home to confirm what I already knew. Instead, after dinner with friends, I hit a downtown gay bar to warm up and drink beer.

Jenna and the apartment friends didn't appreciate my sound logic. They had no intention of sledding of course, but they resented my assumptions so they used my spare key to let themselves into my home and drank all my liquor. They unscrewed light bulbs, froze my toothbrushes, and moved furniture. Rehung photos upside down. Decorated my living room furniture with my dirty laundry. For my welcome-home entertainment, they taped a corn-cob-shaped candle into Plastiqua's hand, wedged it between her squeaky legs, and laid her on top of my bed. She was naked, Senators, so help me, God.

Her presence was like a mafia calling card, less bloody than a horse head but still sinister, suggesting, *when you blow us off for sledding, this is what happens.*

I myself had spent the late-night hours successfully flirting with a tall dark stranger. Said stranger and I decided to turn two hours of vertical chatting into a few hours spent horizontal with decidedly less chatting. When I arrived home very, very late with the raven-haired stranger whom I felt was destined to be my one true love, I ushered my new friend into the dark apartment. I had no idea many pranks had befallen my apartment during my absence and without lights, I guided us toward the back bedroom. I flipped the wall switch, the one light fixture they hadn't disabled.

Behold. There lay Plastiqua, masturbating with a corn cob.

After the initial shock, I howled with laughter.

I couldn't stop.

I laughed and then laughed harder, because I realized when I *stopped* laughing, I would have to explain—to my future true love—why there was a naked blow-up doll in my bed simulating sex.

I eventually managed to squeak out, "That's not mine."

Understandably, he looked surprised.

He glanced at Plastiqua, then me, then the doll. He said, "You said you lived alone."

I started chuckling again, laughter rising up, and said, "I do." Then I laughed for a long time again.

He and I dated for six months. He eventually grew accustomed to Plastiqua's presence at group dinners and may have actually dry humped her once or twice during movie night.

A few years later, Jenna brought Plastiqua to my 30th surprise birthday party wearing a long T-shirt, the kind sexy coeds wear in a horror movie right before they're butchered. Smirking, Jenna whipped out a thick black marker and suggested everyone write birthday messages all over Plastiqua's best and only outfit. Senators, Plastiqua was officially gifted to me that evening. How could I refuse? A few hours (and many drinks) later, a friend sidled up to me and whispered, "I have one photo left in my camera. Do you want a picture of your entire softball team or your dad signing the blow-up doll."

No brainer. How many times does your father sign your inflatable sex doll?

I'd like to say these isolated incidents were the only mishaps with Plastiqua, esteemed Senators, but they were not. Pfft, not even close. If these were Rush Limbaugh scandals, we'd only be current to the early 90s, so buckle up.

One year, I borrowed my best friend Ann's camera when journeying to Rome, Sienna, and Florence. Keep in mind this was a camera from those Amish-like pre-digital days, so when I replenished the film (with actual film), I amused myself considering staging a few photos for Ann to find. Jenna eagerly agreed and we conspired to take four photos of me shirtless getting "caught" in bed with Plastiqua. Wouldn't Ann blush with confusion when the photo worker flashed her a knowing smile? And wouldn't Ann be horrified when she got home, opened her photos, and realized what that employee's knowing smile meant?

Yes, Senators, it backfired.

After three months of unnerving silence and not a single spoken word about the Plastiqua photos, I had assumed Ann and I were silently engaged in a game of chicken, her nerves of steel waiting for me to cave. I kept expecting the Plastiqua photos to show up in my mail, mailed to my folks or something worse, possibly a full-page magazine ad in the local gay paper. I grew a bit paranoid, Senators. I finally broke down one night on the phone. "What about your goddam photos? Why haven't you said anything? I returned the camera *months* ago."

"The camera?" Ann said casually, "Did you still have a few Italy photos on it? I'll tell my mom. I loaned it to her. Funny coincidence. She called me last night to tell me she was getting the photos developed today."

You know what, Senators? Forget it.

This setting the record straight isn't working out to my advantage. I mean, there are *more* stories, more inappropriateness with Plastiqua. Given my record of public humiliations, it's a marvel I'm not agoraphobic, but honestly, being inside my house isn't any safer from these ongoing indignities.

Case in point.

Two years after Jenna moved to Boston, she emailed me her intention to return to the Twin Cities for a short visit. I promised to bring Plastiqua for Jenna's and my reunion dinner, but sadly our plastic friend had gotten punctured in a storage box in my basement (ironically, her first *real* hole), so I inflated her and drowned her in the bathtub (Plastiqua, not Jenna) to let air bubbles guide me where to apply the fix-it Band-Aid. I forgot this mid-morning drowning and launched three other house projects which distracted me.

I had a lunch date a few blocks from my apartment, a first date with a fellow I had met online, so I strolled to the Italian café in warm sunlight. During lunch with my future true love, I offered to loan him a book, a clear-cut signal I liked him and wanted to see him again. He came back to my place to retrieve the book as a clear-cut sign he liked me and wanted to see me again. Predictably enough, he asked to use the bathroom.

"Sure, sure," I said.

After the toilet flushed and a curiously long time passed while he washed his hands, he emerged, visibly shaken. "There's a naked lady floating in your bath tub."

"Oh, right," I said in a nonchalant voice. "Her."

At some point, you become inured to your own scandals; they hardly sound terrible to your own ears. See, Senators, I get you. I really really do.

DEAR PENTHOUSE,

AS A chubby teen, I was introduced to your letter column through a high school friend's sleepover. He titillated our boys club by showing us his father's stash. We poured over them. The other boys were mesmerized by all the pictures of women spreading their legs. I was mesmerized by the naughty cartoons and also the letters written by men who experienced surprising seductions. I loved those masculine, sexy letters. I ignored the icky photos and devoured how the men felt, the raw pleasure of seduction and getting sex delivered so easily, like pizza. Well, sometimes *literally* through a pizza delivery woman. Later, as the other boys moved to another room to play Atari video games, I remained behind, reading your letters, studying them. So I know exactly how to begin.

Dear Penthouse, this kind of situation doesn't ever happen to me. (I nailed it, right?) I'm not the guy who gets hit on at parties. I'm the guy you ask, "Dude, where's the beer?" Hot neighbors don't wash their Corvettes in tight jeans cutoffs for me and I've never had a voluptuous male tutor make sexy double entendres while I was labored over Italian vocabulary. Mostly my tutors spent their energy suppressing frustration because my brain refused verb conjugation.

Penthouse letters are traditionally crammed full of clichés, so allow me to say you could have knocked me over with a feather when my own Penthouse experience showed up at my front door one weeknight after 10 p.m. The pounding roused me from writing in my den, which was the first irritation and as

I crossed to the front of the house, I couldn't help but complain. My porch light and living room lights were already off. Who ignores those obvious signs?

Grumble, grumble.

The pounding resumed a second time, already impatient with me.

I was not amused.

I peered through glass planes like the crabby ass I felt myself to be and was surprised to see Mike. He was one of three twenty-somethings renting the house next door. His two housemates, both women, were bubbly and friendly to me, contrasting his surliness. Maybe they were compensating. I knew he was a homo the day I met him. Shaking hands, he looked at me and his entire face wrinkled into mild disgust, as if to communicate, *Ugh. Bear.*

Mike dressed casually but with great attention to detail and he affected a beard which looked scraggly on him in his post-twink era. His hair bristled with chemical product and always remained sculpted to look as if it were not. The modern word best describing Mike is *hipster* but back in the mid-2000s, we had not yet dreamt up that new-fangled vernacular to define someone who tries hard to make you believe he doesn't care about his appearance. Mike himself would boast he was a hipster before it was cool.

His cheerful housemates and I would sometimes gab if we came home at the same time, twelve-sentence conversations as we lugged our gym bags and groceries to our front doors. Mike never said more than hello and sometimes only shot me a grim nod if he could not avoid eye contact. No problem. Not everybody has to be chat buddies in the front yard but since he had never come to my home in the two years living next door, I was mighty alarmed to find him standing on my front porch.

When I opened the door, he said, "You know, we've never really gotten to know each other as neighbors."

I said, "No, I guess not."

For him, that must have translated into, *Well then, come the fuck in*, because that's what he did, sailing across the threshold and squeezing past me, clearly propelled forward by the thick alcohol cloud surrounding him. I thought I might get wasted by proxy.

He dropped on my living room couch, the big one, and I sat across from him, a three-by-four-foot oak coffee table between us. I briefly wondered if this could be a booty call but that seemed absurd as he made it a habit to scowl at me. He had probably locked himself out and needed to waste a half hour before a housemate came home. If he had just glared at me and said, "Look, I'm locked out. Can I crash here until my roommate gets home?" that would have been fine. In fact, I would have preferred the honesty.

Mike asked, "Got anything to drink?"

I tried to hide my annoyance when I said, "I'll check."

My kitchen was a disaster, dirty dishes everywhere and leftover carnage from dinner suggesting I'm not the kind of person who uses my hands to open packages and move things around. While I take pleasure in believing I'm a free spirit who doesn't mind if my household is cluttered and dirty when friends spontaneously visit, sorry, I'm really not. I do not appreciate chicken gravy on most flat kitchen surfaces and scum-riddled plates piling up like a high-rise buffet for rats. In moments like this, I hear my mother's voice say, "That's why we make our bed every morning and do the dishes after each meal, because you never know who may drop by."

I don't think she anticipated booty calls, however.

Of course, Mike strolled into the mess right behind me and when he (deliberately?) brushed against me, I inhaled a full shot glass of whiskey breath or something of equivalent proof. He nodded at the vodka sitting on top of my fridge and noted it would serve fine. (I store my hard liquor on top the fridge. Mine is not the classiest house even when it's clean.)

I grumbled while I found us clean glasses, wondering how long this stupid seduction would take. If it were that. I still wasn't sure.

It sucks when you're getting your Penthouse experience, the young neighbor almost twenty years your junior appearing suddenly for a booty call, and all you can think is *God, I am turning into my mother.*

When we returned to the Mission-style couches in my cozy Minneapolis bungalow, I sat where he was not so he moved and joined me on my couch. He sat very, very close and asked, "Do you have a boyfriend?"

Yup. Booty call.

"Yes, I do," I said right away. "It's not an open relationship."

He frowned. "Oh. I never see him."

"We mostly sleep at his place."

As I scooched a few inches away, keeping a more appropriate distance between us, I elaborated. The relationship was fairly new, that delicate stage where no one uttered the word *monogamy*, but wouldn't it feel great if we both shared that shy desire? Wouldn't the timing be nice? I told a sweet tale of my new boyfriend and our potential for being each other's one true love.

None of it was true. I was very, very single and actually lacking in amorous adventures of late (which is a classy way of saying I was horny).

But when Mike switched couches and I felt the heat of his body as he dropped next to me, I had decided *no way* and instantly lies poured from my mouth regarding this newish romance while my brain screamed, "For God's sake, don't give him a fake name! You'll never remember it."

"Things are good right now between him and me," I said, purring. "Who knows where it will go. You dating anyone?"

"No," he said staring into my eyes, "Single."

He moved his hand to massage the back of my neck.

This moment, my lie, was one of those questionable decisions a person makes in life. Why didn't I go for it? We were both single, he was attractive, just sort of scornful and pretentious. I didn't like him as a person but he wasn't proposing six hours of conversation. Why did I invent this big lie? Why not just get laid, consequences be damned?

I removed his massaging hand and realized I truly didn't want this, not with him. Maybe there comes a point in your life where respecting yourself finally overtakes the need for carnival sex. Maybe. I'm a big fan of carnival sex. I got my hand stamped so I can come back anytime. But I don't spend my every waking moment wondering about who might be next or thinking about what we might try.

"I'd like to see your house," he said, "see how it compares to ours."

The rest of my house wasn't much cleaner than the food-splattered kitchen, so he wasn't winning any points with me by demanding to see every room in its natural state. But I wanted us off the romantic couch so I walked him room to room. When we headed through the kitchen toward the sun porch he embraced me from behind and kissed me on the neck.

I froze. Why the kitchen? Couldn't he see the mess? The chicken gravy? I couldn't possibly make out with all those dirty dishes mocking me from a foot away.

"I know you want me," he whispered in sloppy dramatic seduction. "I see you watching me from your house. From your kitchen you can see right into my bedroom."

I extracted myself and said, "Mike, I don't even know which room is yours. I've never been in your house to know that."

He pointed to his window and said, "That one. I know you watch me undress. I see you standing right here."

I pondered this and said, "Huh."

I had never watched him undress. I really didn't know which room was his. But I knew why he would think I might have.

Mike wasn't entirely wrong. I did spend a lot of time in this spot, just not for the reason he suspected.

I decided to tell the truth. Another questionable decision.

"Thing is," I said and I probably blushed a little, "we're right in front of the refrigerator. I spend *a lot* of time at the fridge with the door open. Standing right here."

That was humiliating.

It can be hard to tell your embarrassing truths, like why I spend so much time in front of the fridge debating meal options, or why I am single. Well-meaning friends frequently ask with loving concern why I'm still single, and while my defenses can offer a variety of reasons from "I'm not putting myself out there" to "I'm concentrating on my writing these days," sometimes the truth is "I don't know. I guess I don't really know."

He tried to kiss me again and I said, "No. No, Mike."

Man, this Penthouse letter sucked.

We continued the house tour and now that it seemed apparent he wasn't getting laid, he didn't fake being impressed by each room. In the den he looked at my festive Christmas lights wrapping a house plant and said with disdain, "Oh. *So* tacky."

After we concluded the downstairs, the only part of my house tour available to the visiting public, he strode past me in the dining room and asked, "What's up here?"

He disappeared up the narrow staircase into my master bedroom.

I followed, not liking where this was headed symbolically or literally. I was sure my imaginary boyfriend would raise his eyebrow when I repeated this part of the story, doubting for a moment whether we were truly heading toward the monogamous thing after all. Thank God, I did not give the imaginary boyfriend a name. I'd never remember it.

I found what I expected to find, underwear and shirts on the floor, comic books strewn about, pomegranate-striped sheets rumpled at the foot of my bed, my pillows slammed and drooping against far walls as if my sleep violence ought to be studied in a lab.

There he was, lying on my unmade bed, flipping through a comic book.

And *this* is why we make our bed every morning.

The cupboard door to my secret stash of unread comics stood wide open and he had reached in, grabbed a random book. He wore his natural state of disdain on his face, flipping through the colored pages.

My blood hardened in its veins. You don't fuck with a nerd's comics, dude. Not cool.

"C'mon," I said with forced good cheer, "I still haven't shown you the basement."

When my tour completed its run and I walked us to the front door, he resisted and flopped onto my living room couch again for one final attempt at seduction. He patted the seat next to him and I murmured, "My boyfriend."

In a bored voice he asked me what I did for fun and I said, "I write."

He said, "Me too. I'm a blogger."

This became the only *I'll show you mine if you show me yours* moment of the night, for we each whipped out our home pages on my laptop and ogled them, right there on the oak coffee table. As expected, he saw my homepage and said, "Yeah, that's nice. Here's mine."

I never expected any real interest from him. I was a booty call.

"I'm new to blogging," he confessed.

His blog had two entries on it, *only* two, and both began with rants against junk food manufacturers and their stupidity. His written attitude was a mixture of confidence-without-facts and everyone-is-stupid, so while he explained his theme for colors and layout, I grew more irritated with him and felt a resolve in myself to get rid of him within the next five minutes.

"I'm anorexic," Mike said. "Well, recovering anorexic. Not many men get diagnosed with anorexia compared to women, so I felt my voice needed to be out there."

I looked at his blog posts again and instead of seeing smug confidence I saw a defiant, wounded man still struggling to succeed. When you uncover a vulnerable dimension to a late-night booty call, it's suddenly harder to think of him exclusively as a booze-guzzling jerk.

I listened to him describe his relationship with food and I told him he was brave, which he was, and he responded with a knowing smile to suggest, *Yeah, I really am.* Okay, I still didn't like him. But I could appreciate before me I beheld a man on a journey, same as me.

Dear Penthouse, I sent Mike home a few minutes later after he suggested my imaginary boyfriend never had to know about this. Mike let me know we didn't have to do *everything*, but maybe just *some* things. I made sure he crossed safely to his own front door and made a mental note to spend less time at the fridge. Jesus, what if he gave me a deliberate striptease while I was salivating over leftover lasagna?

The next morning after the Penthouse seduction, the UPS man asked if I could sign for an important package for my female next-door neighbors. Working from home as I did, my signing for neighbor packages was not unusual. I left a note taped to their front door to come over.

I considered he might be the one to come, but the odds were against it. Besides, it might be healing for both of us to acknowledge the previous night's awkwardness, laugh about it, get it out there, and—crap. I couldn't remember if I had assigned my imaginary boyfriend a name. I hoped not. I hope I had taken my own advice, but I don't always listen to the voice inside me which says, "Not a good idea."

Two hours later, I recognized Mike's impatient pounding on the front door, like a British soldier checking American homes during the Revolutionary War.

I opened the screen door wide so he could enter and in a sheepish voice, I said, "Hi."

He took the package from my hand and flashed me the familiar scorn: *Ugh. Bear.*

In a bored voice he said, "Thanks for signing for this."

Mike turned and plopped down the front steps in a casual way. Obviously, last night's rejection did not scar him.

That was it. That was the end of our rich, meaningful relationship. A year later, he moved away.

Dear Penthouse, nothing happened.

Okay, well, not technically true. The prior night, we made out for a minute by my front door as I was sending him home, but then I whispered, "I can't. The boyfriend," and kicked him out.

What? Don't judge me.

I'm not made of stone and this was probably going to be my only Penthouse experience.

WHEN WE WERE BRAVE

LAST WEEK, as I snorkeled out to a sunken ship in the Caribbean Sea, two thoughts emerged: first, this is the bravest thing I have ever done, and second, I can't wait to get home and write a blog post that begins: last week, as I snorkeled out to a sunken ship in the Caribbean Sea....

Ann and I vacationed to Mexico, a beach vacation in a remote spot along the Yucatan Peninsula. She is much braver about travel and committing to plans, so in January I took her seriously when she said with excitement, "Mexico, baby!"

She travels the world because she's interested in other cultures, other cities, other people. I'm interested too, but it's easier to read about people and cultures on Wikipedia. I find traveling requires a certain bravery, a confidence details will simply work themselves out. Almost 15 years ago as I fussed over what to take with me to Italy, Ann told me, "The only things you need are good walking shoes and a credit card. Everything else you can buy."

She was right.

Last Sunday, when we didn't find each other immediately in the Cancun airport, I panicked. When I finally reached Ann by phone, I was borderline hyperventilating, stranded in a foreign country, and she answered her phone cheerfully, saying, "Hey, how ya doing?" She wasn't flustered in the slightest. Everything would work out. She *makes* things work out, which is why she's the perfect traveling companion.

Four days later, we found ourselves following our resort owner's recommendation to drive deep into a Mexican jungle, find a certain unmarked road to a deserted beach, and then stroll down the beach to reach swimming distance to the sunken ship's bow, our snorkeling destination.

Marsha, our resort host, promised no people would be around. She said this as if it were a good thing, whereas I could only picture me being dragged into the ocean by a giant squid and Ann yelling, "Shark! Shark!" but nobody would be around to help. (This point may have been moot, but I hoped Ann would have the common sense to yell "Shark! Shark!" because, really, who's going to come running for "Squid! Squid!")

Despite Marsha's description, we decided to be brave, to have this adventure.

As we drove deeper and deeper through Mexican jungle, we laughed ourselves silly about how if we got lost, nobody would ever—could ever—find us. After all, our small resort was located eighteen kilometers down a gravel road in an already sparsely populated part of Mexico. No cell coverage, no nearby convenience stores, no neighboring towns. The hotel enjoyed electricity for only six hours a day and we showered with collected rainwater. When Marsha described the sunken ship spot as remote, Ann and I glanced at each other nervously. We thought we were already experiencing remote.

In the jungle, Jurassic Park did not seem a far-fetched concept, so much as a logical extension of the landscape. The car bounced along a road only classified as a road because ruts suggested other cars had driven on it. Trees branches and brush pressed hard against the car and we grew quiet.

We kept our eyes peeled for crocodiles, iguanas, small foxes, car-eating snakes, and other creatures. Aloud, we wondered what would happen if we actually witnessed wildlife. Hands gripping the steering wheel tightly, I decided I would most likely leap from the car and punch said crocodile in the head repeatedly, just to show him who was boss. Ann listened politely to my exaggerated brags and during my speech, she pointed and quietly said, "Croc." I swerved the car in terror.

Studying Marsha's homemade map, we counted kilometers until we found the unmarked turnoff, and parked the car near someone's assembled collection of assorted driftwood and corrugated aluminum, possibly someone's abandoned home. Two growling, snarling dogs greeted us, and Ann and I looked at each other dubiously. Although I do not speak Mexican dog, I caught the gist: drive away now or we will rip your fucking calves off.

We could see half the ship emerging from the water, a good quarter mile away from us.

"Still want to do this?" I asked.

"Sure!" she said.

Of course she did.

Reasonable people would make a pact to *not* do this and simply lie to all their friends back home. Take pictures from the shore, swear we swam out there, talk about how gorgeous the water was, so warm, so many fish, etc. Reasonable people wouldn't make each other, you know, actually *do* it.

But Ann is brave.

That's not to say she doesn't get scared—she does. We talk on the phone when she's afraid and she tells me about these fears. And yet, whatever it is that's scaring her, she often does it anyway. After fifteen years of marriage, she started life over in Iowa to pursue a PhD. Upon completion, she moved to North Carolina, ready to start over again. Professionally, she keeps extending herself, risking, challenging, pushing. She seeks out gifted children in poorer urban schools, the ones where most people see only high-risk students. She hunts a different treasure from most and she frequently finds it. In her personal life, she examines her own motives and actions with an unflinching flashlight, and when she uncovers answers she does not like, she says, "Well, shit."

Some days, when she grows weary from pushing the world to be a better place, or tired of pushing herself, she can't see the immense bravery I see. When we talk on those days, she feels broken. But I am not fooled. I recognize courage, even if its voice is hurt and small.

When we refused to leave the desolate beach, the snarling dogs relented.

Like so many of us in life, they used their bark to mask their desire for love and were afraid we would not give it. I knelt in the sand. One trotted closer, head bowed, asking for forgiveness. Instantly, we loved Scooter. (And if you saw this adorable beach mutt, you would know right off his name had to be Scooter or the Mexican equivalent of Scooter.) He had happy eyes and a deep scar across his schnoz that made me feel sad for his past fights. When we invited him to accompany us on our walk down the beach, he wagged his tail eagerly, zipping between our legs and running ahead of us, looking back as if to say, "C'mon! This way!"

I fantasized about smuggling him back to Minnesota. I have no doubt Scooter would protest leaving this gorgeous, tropical location. He was probably quite happy here. But I loved him and wanted him to winter with me.

We attached our flippers with typical comical results, falling over in the surf, more sand in our butt cracks, spitting salt water-infused laughter out the breathing tubes. Scooter raced around our belongings on the beach as if promising to protect them. We promised him pretzels and water upon our return to the car.

As we dunked ourselves into deeper water, I wondered if Ann felt afraid or was this no big deal for her. Right before we started swimming, I removed my breathing tube and said, "Marsha said it was unlikely sharks come into water this shallow."

Ann said, "Let's hope the sharks remember that."

In the clear water, we swam near fish with neon blue ridges, shimmering spectacles who darted away easily, tiny silver sprinters, and big fatties that looked at us with surprise: what the hell are *you* doing here? We pointed out favorite fish to each other, oranges, impossible yellows, and more of the silver sprinters, my favorites.

The farther we swam out, the waves pushed harder. But we kept going, floating with intentional direction. Beautiful coral met us, delicate purple constructions of exquisite lace perched on orange reefs. We found violet fish, fish with green stripes blending into the underwater grass, blue and yellow-stripers, and really, where the hell was Sebastian from *The Little Mermaid*?

I always forget there is a payoff for bravery.

As we swam out further, I remembered times I was brave: quitting a job, saying no to a boss, telling a friend, "I think you're messed up." I have been brave with cancer, brave in a grocery store, brave with strangers, and even with lovers, brave enough to say, "I'm not happy." I remember a devastating fight with Ann many years ago, facing my fears our friendship might not survive. Reeling in hurt and surprise we both required bravery as we negotiated our reconciliation.

We eventually reached the sunken ship.

An enormous pelican—big enough to sit on my chest and make me gasp for air—perched on the stern, eyeing us with suspicion. Though we splashed around pretty close, it refused to surrender its position. I swear I could see its feathers trembling and I thought, "It's brave, too."

I found myself disappointed in the ship itself, the rusted metal frame completely lacking in skull and crossbones decoration. While I recognized it was unrealistic to hope for a treasure chest with gold coins spilling out, still, I nurtured the tiniest hope that maybe...just maybe...

Nope.

With the surf pushing us harder toward shore and simultaneously trying to seduce us deeper, it did not take long for Ann and I to say, "Okay, we've seen it."

We snorkeled back, stopping to swim around orange coral reefs and admire our swim mates.

Once on shore, we were disappointed to find Scooter had deserted us. As we collected our flippers and headed back to the car, I asked Ann if this was the bravest thing she had ever done.

"Yes," she said immediately. "No wait, getting divorced was first. This is second."

Today, sitting in my overstuffed chair upstairs in my cozy bedroom with a Diet Coke at my side, I look at the photo of our sunken ship and I think the caption should be: When We Were Brave.

FOND MEMORIES OF THE MANHOLE

DESPITE THE ominous title, this essay is rated PG-13 for strong language. No nudity. There is one furious drag queen screaming in front of a Chicago leather bar, so yes, adult situations.

Two weeks ago, on a return trip to visit family, I wandered up and down Chicago's Halsted Street, lost in reminiscing. I remembered dining at that narrow but long restaurant when it was Italian and not a French/Vietnamese cafe. I hung out a few times in that cruddy little bar when it proudly bore the name of the previous bar owner. It was a cruddy little bar then, too. I remembered some first dates, some last dates. A couple landmarks changed over the years but The Alley and that excellent comic book shop remained, as well as the Belmont Street Dunkin' Donuts.

Glad to see that.

I was disappointed to observe the Manhole, a raunchy leather bar, had gentrified into something classier and pastel sounding: a bar called Hydrate. Although it was never a hangout of mine, still, I missed the Manhole. One sunny afternoon, I fought the most wonderful, physically abusive, domestic argument outside that bar.

At the time I lived in a northwest suburb and on weekends volunteered for a Boystown group called the Pink Angels. In response to that late-80s take-back-the-city movement, Chicago's Pink Angels copied other successful groups' mission and patrolled the predominantly gay neighborhood. Pink

Angels jogged down dark alleys reporting drug deals to cops, helped drunks find cabs, and ran like hell toward any cry sounding like "Help!"

It takes a unique flavor of compassion to love people this way, to race to their aid down a dark alley. Groups patrolled from about 10 p.m. until 4 a.m. on Friday and Saturday nights. For one summer, I was a member but it turns out I am chunky and there was a lot of running involved. Still, for one summer, I ran the streets of Chicago.

We wore pink T-shirts and matching berets. I thank Hercules this happened prior to phone cameras' popularity for I did not project "sexy strong gay" in my pink beret. I was a pink-tinged, jolly cake topper you'd stick on a German chocolate cake for a child's first communion celebration. We never engaged in true fisticuffs that summer (which is smart—some of us undoubtedly imagined West Side Story and would have been mightily surprised when our attackers did not bring tap shoes), but I felt brave among them. I felt safe.

In the heat of August, we conducted training for the new recruits. After morning workshops on walking tough, non-confrontational de-escalation and how to observe street-smart nuances, the experienced volunteers broke into small groups to enact training situations around a ten-block radius.

My assignment was to stage a domestic argument in front of the Manhole. Our training director set the scene: I was to be witnessed verbally harassing and physically intimidating my assigned boyfriend in the bar's front entryway, screaming at him, and he would, in turn, give the appropriate signs of intimidation, subtle and skillfully done. The Pink Angels would approach and demand to know if everything was okay.

Portraying the brutish thug, I would execute my line with menacing undertones. "He's fine. Go away."

The Pink Angels would insist on hearing from my partner. He would respond by saying, "It's okay," in an unconvincing tone. They might ask again for a clearer answer. I would stand close to him, pinning my boyfriend against the Manhole's exterior, my arm blocking a view to his face. When they reluctantly withdrew and moved a few feet away, I would give him a hearty shove, which would trigger scene two: the dramatic return and de-escalation to remove me from the man I intended to beat down.

Our roles clear, my new life partner and I looked at each other, shrugged, and said, "Sure. We can do this."

As we walked toward the Manhole together, we exchanged names and short bio information. He lived in Chicago proper and while he expressed admiration for the greatness of Arlington Heights, he clearly looked down on me as a suburb dweller.

North Halsted was crowded, the regular Saturday flow of people living in north side Chicago, shopping, strolling, jogging, or generally fucking around under the hot August sun. The Pink Angels would not show for a few minutes, so we practiced my pushing him in a way that didn't hurt but still looked realistic. I practiced yelling mean things. About three minutes before our patrol was due, during a faux shoving, we both jumped to hear a rich baritone voice four feet behind me.

"Oh bitch, you did *not* just shove that man."

We both turned sheepishly to find a 6'2" African-American drag queen with her hands on her hips. She wore a leopard print miniskirt and had big RuPaul hair. She would claw my eyes out for not remembering her top, but I was so stunned I forgot to check out her breasts.

I was about to get my ass kicked.

"He's fine," I said in a pleading voice. Thinking the patrol could be here at any second, I added, "Go away."

When she started yelling at me, threatening me, moving closer, I turned to my temporary boyfriend and said, "Tell her."

In a completely unconvincing tone, he said, "It's okay."

On the plus side, we had accidentally practiced our lines and he hit the mark perfectly as unbelievable and in danger. I, on the other hand, could have used more authority in saying, "Go away."

One or two people stopped to watch as she swore loudly. I tried to explain we represented the Pink Angels training team and could she please not let them find me spread-eagle on the sticky, scalding sidewalk with her black stiletto heel jammed into my fleshy neck. She was furious. Nervously, we did our best to persuade her.

Our furtive glances down the street in the direction of our soon-to-be-arriving patrol apparently lent more credibility than our actual words and she reluctantly agreed to step back a few feet. But she let me know she was *not* departing until this alleged training scenario played out and if I thought I could outrun a bitch in heels, I had another thing coming.

"Please," I begged her. "Stand far enough away. Over there."

She skulked away, but not far.

My partner and I got into position and we took a few deep breaths because the lady was not shy with swear words and could threaten some explicit possibilities. It takes a different kind of courage to be a Chicago drag queen.

"They're almost here," my faux-boyfriend said, eyes wide. "Go. Do your thing."

"Don't fucking tell me what to do you piece of *shit*," I yelled in his face, jabbing a hard forefinger two inches from his eyes.

The Pink Angels appeared at my side and we played out our scene. My partner was said he was okay (unconvincingly, of course) so they reluctantly retreated. I shoved my faux-boyfriend with faux-rage. They returned and dragged me away using the proper techniques, though I had a few critique notes to pass along once we debriefed at headquarters. If anyone on the patrol team paid deeper attention, they would have noticed I was probably the more rattled of the two actors.

By the time the Pink Angels had resolved our drama and began jogging to the next scene, our drag queen had silently slipped away.

This is what I love about Chicago.

If you're in a shop and overhear a conversation that's not meant for your ears, chime in. It's still your fuckin' business. This city is where I learned to tell drunks, "Get out of my face!" and how to get seen when howling for a cab. If you think you're gonna knock your boyfriend's teeth out, you may have to answer to a self-policing pack of homos in matching pink berets or an African-American goddess who is not going to stand for any shit.

On the day I walked Halsted reminiscing, my fond memories from the Manhole were enough to make me want to stand at the corner of Belmont and North Clark, and, ala Mary Tyler Moore, throw a pink beret into the air screaming, "*Fuck you, Chicago.*"

I have no doubt someone, whether in a brownstone, at the Dunkin' Donuts, or from the back seat of a cab, would yell back, "No, fuck *you*! What's your fucking problem?"

And they'd really want to know.

200 WORDS OR LESS, PLEASE

MY PUBLISHING house recently tasked me with writing my author biography.

I was tickled. Thrilled, even. I had been eagerly waiting for the professional need to write this. Huzzah! My book was getting published! But as I sat before the softly glowing screen staring at my fingers hovering above the keyboard, ready to sum my relationship with writing in 200 words or less (and in third person), I found myself lost.

I experimented with different approaches.

First, I tried a historical approach:

Edmond Manning has been writing for many years, but his first works of fiction were simply atrocious. Seriously. Should you have been unfortunate enough to encounter any of the over-exclamation-pointed drivel, you would not purchase this book you're currently considering. Which you should. Purchase it, that is, because those over-exclamated days are behind him!!

That reflected a little too much humiliating honesty (not to mention didn't even come close to using 200 words), so I tried the out-and-out bragging approach:

Edmond spent years studying literary masterpieces and more recently attended the University of Iowa's renowned Writers' Workshop. Using only pen and quill, he conquered the craft from granular sentence construction to the loftiest thematic structures by European greats, all in service to realizing potent, melodic paragraphs designed to make you weep openly, laugh heartily, and then go purchase a silk handkerchief for the mere purpose of throwing at his feet like a true Victorian homeboy.

It was only 75 words.

Also, it was chock full of lies.

"Years studying literary masterpieces" meant I spent my lonely teenage years reading every Charles Dickens book I could devour in my bedroom. I only attended a one-week summer seminar through the Iowa Writers' Workshop, available to anyone with a checkbook, where I listened to estate lawyers sick of their profession argue about whether good abs was a character-defining trait.

I needed a different approach. Why was this so challenging?

I wrote novels for twenty-plus years but honestly, for most of that time never took writing seriously. I felt objective enough to realize my fiction was high-end mediocre, certainly not publishable. (Ann, my awesome friend and all-time cheerleader, often disagreed. She is wonderful.) While I definitely *wanted* my writing to register as amazing and even entertained fantasies involving around-the-block lines for my book signings, I can't say I developed a serious plan to make fantasy become reality. (However, I did practice my fruity, author signature.)

I took a writing class here and there. Wrote a hundred pages. Realized it was crap. Repeated.

My former neighbor Jenna had similar aspirations but much to my surprise, she actually did something about it. She pursued a creative writing master degree from a prestigious university, and then launched a writing career. I didn't know you could do that—*make* yourself better and go after what you wanted. She did.

I watched her growing success with a detached curiosity and wondered why I did not share that same drive, that internal passion bleating, *I want this more than anything.*

I took another writing class. Wrote another hundred pages. The results were...meh.

I knew I hadn't committed to becoming an author. But did I want it enough? Or would I eventually regret not giving writing my everything? What if my undiscovered gift was jazz solos on the saxophone and I had not yet unearthed that particular talent? How do you know when you found your *thing*?

Through it all, I enjoyed myself. I liked finding unusual stories, mapping hilarious conversations, and designing unique approaches to characters. Still, I didn't see myself as a writer, not really. Where was my passion?

In 2008, I wrote a short story about something not terribly important to me but important to a closeted 20-year-old gay man I met online. He felt sad and alone. I remembered those days and decided he needed inspiration, so I wrote him a short story featuring a happier version of him as the lead character and uploaded it on a free website. This was my personalized It Gets Better project before Dan Savage's amazing It Gets Better project. I decided to try a few literary tricks, fuck with the point of view, toss in masculine archetypes, some Joseph Campbell shit, because why the fuck not? Who cared? It was merely a writing exercise to cheer up an online friend whom I would never meet.

Because I wasn't writing SERIOUS FICTION I dropped all expectations (i.e. literary pretensions) and a curious thing happened. The story flowed through me, relaxed and intentional. Decade after decade of sweeping out mediocre sentences paid off, transforming my writing with surprising grace into a Cinderella story, a lyrical, ball-gown construction resulting in beautiful sentences. I wrote *beautiful sentences*. I really, really liked what I wrote.

So I wrote more. Uploaded to the free website. Added another chapter, this one about kings, a tribe I called the Lost and Founds.

Emails from readers began pouring in. First dozens, then hundreds. Men and women from Europe, Africa, and quite a few from the United States. People mailed me gifts. Through this experience, I found an amazing editor, a retired professional who now mentored writers she collected from various experiences. She saw my fiction and emailed me to say, "It's time for you to get published." I reeled in shock from the impact these stories created and how individuals attempted to integrate my fiction into their reality.

A shopkeeper in France, a woman in her late twenties, emailed to explain how she tried "the king's kiss" on an elderly customer, kissing the palm of his hand, and how he started to cry with gratitude at such kindness.

Writing this fiction, this throwaway story of kings unleashed a fire, a passion I had no idea was kindling inside me. In trying to describe my 2008 writing phenomenon, I've referenced romantic comedies where the protagonist suddenly realizes he's been in love with his best friend all these years, and so he races to break up an impending wedding. I'm not sure I could run to the church without ending up wheezing and huffing, hunched over, but still, it mostly fits.

I *love* writing fiction.

I feel lucky to have fallen in love with my best friend of twenty-some years, and foolish when I consider how long it took me to arrive here. (One of the first things I did was to call Jenna and say, "I get it now. I want this more than anything.") In my 'Probably Shouldn't Have Done This' list of regrets I would add waiting to throw all my love at this casual hobby of mine.

This is what I submitted to my publisher.

Edmond Manning has always been fascinated by fiction: how ordinary words could be sculpted into heartfelt emotions, how heartfelt emotions could leave an imprint inside you stronger than the real world. Manning never felt worthy to tread down these hallowed halls as an author until recently, when he accidentally stumbled into his own writer's voice that fit well like his favorite skull-print, fuzzy jammies. He finally realized he didn't have to adopt the style of Charles Dickens or Armistead Maupin, two author heroes, and perhaps his own insignificant writing was perfect because it was his true voice, so he looked around the scrappy word kingdom he created for himself and shouted, "I'M HOME!" He is now a writer.

That was 118 words.

It could work.

TO ALL MY MKP BROTHERS, ESPECIALLY THE STRAIGHT ONES

I HAD a toothbrush in my mouth and was contemplating sleep when my overnight guest, a straight man, said to me, "I have a real problem with gay men."

As a gay man, hearing this statement from a man I voluntarily agreed to shelter overnight was not exactly comforting. Was this the beginning of an ugly conflict? What hard words might come out next?

I should back up.

Minnesota's local chapter of the ManKind Project (MKP) produced a weekend training workshop. Locals and out-of-staters showed up to sit around the metaphorical campfire and discuss our New Warrior Training Adventure weekend and the raw guts of who we are as men. Those of us with spare rooms offered weekend housing. I agreed to host a fellow Minnesotan named Joe who lived outside the Twin Cities area. I knew Joe, but not well.

Over multiple New Warrior Training Adventure staffings, Joe and I interacted regularly. We liked each other well enough but he kept me at a distance and I respected it. After a few staffings where we collaborated well, Joe and I decided to expand on our mutual trust by partnering to facilitate some emotional work in a third man.

On these powerful, transformational MKP weekends you don't choose to partner with another staff man unless you trust he can watch your back. Doesn't matter if it's his first staffing or thirtieth—it's not always about experience. It's about the man. You don't partner unless can you stare into that man's eyes and communicate, *Together,* we *can handle this. We can go there.*

After the Friday night training, Joe volunteered to stay at my house. I set him up in his guest bedroom, gave him towels and offered up the contents of my fridge. Host stuff. We were tired and Saturday promised to be a long day. I was brushing my teeth and simultaneously watering house plants because I never just brush my teeth. I multitask. As we said our goodnights, I finished brushing and my toothbrush still dangled from my mouth.

Joe stood up from the living room couch and asked me to wait, please wait. He was quiet for a moment, uncomfortable.

Finally, he said, "I have a real problem with gay men."

I froze.

A younger version of me would have already knifed an angry retort. But New Warriors frequently smash into each other at that amazing intersection of testosterone and vulnerability and we often come out better for the collision. So, I waited. Joe continued to speak.

He said, "I would like to understand more about this. I think you're the man to help me."

We looked each other in the eyes and silently communicated, *Together, we can go there.*

We sat.

We talked.

I won't pretend it wasn't awkward or tense. It was. It was hard for me to be the warrior he needed while he did his work; I tried not getting triggered by my own shit. We followed those basic but effective communication guidelines regarding I-statements and owning shadowy perceptions as they emerged. Gently, we called bullshit on each other as needed. *Gently.*

Joe asked questions. He didn't understand why gay men did certain things.

We talked cautiously and late into the night, sharing our hearts, hearing each other's story with the listening reserved for men you want to know better. Men you might love in your deepest heart of hearts if you first navigate tricky terrain together.

In the end, Joe concluded, "I still don't get it. I don't *get* gay dudes. How can you not want to have sex with a woman? I mean, how is it possible you aren't totally turned on by women? I don't understand."

"That's okay," I said. "Who said you had to totally understand being gay? It's enough you tried. You're into women. End of story."

He was shocked, relieved and delighted. While he contemplated my answer, I confessed I didn't understand his attraction to women, the physical part. I'm all over the emotional attraction and I love the women in my life. I simply do not *get* the sex part. It's not me.

As we talked deeper, turns out Joe, who is a handsome guy, was repeatedly hit on over the years by aggressive gay men who viewed him as a tasty treat and decided to go for it. Gay men attempted to seduce him with the upsetting logic, "If you were open-minded about gays, you'd try the sex, really just experiment with the sex to better understand gays...."

In short, gay men disrespected him. Over and over. They did not honor his sexuality by leaving him alone. As a result he felt like shit for not trying harder to understand gays but there was no fucking way he would ever try *that*. I had given him permission to *not* understand being gay and it was a revelation for him.

This late-night conversation is a perfect representation of masculine magic—we untangle shit together, the ugly marriage of hurt and negativity, of stereotyping and raging. We men untangle knots. Turns out, only a gay man could untangle that mess for Joe and quite frankly, he had had enough of the gays. Until his New Warrior Training Adventure experience, Joe had little interest in befriending another gay man.

But he reconsidered.

After that night, Joe and I staffed retreat weekends as close friends, loving each other in the way male friends can. One weekend, after one particularly grueling piece of emotional work involving a shitty, shitty father, Joe and I took each other outside and wept together. At the onset of another staff weekend, I was feeling whimsical and introduced myself as Joe's biological brother. Whenever someone called out his last name, we both stood and I said, "Which brother did you want—him or me?" Joe loved it. For that weekend, we were *truly* brothers.

When Joe became a father, he beamed from the inside out, showing off pictures of his newborn son. Whenever his love for his young family shone through him, Joe was the most handsome father and woman-loving man who ever walked the earth. To encounter him was to behold a man made of sunlight.

We're mostly Facebook buddies these days, but every now and then we connect in a meaningful way and I suspect we will always be go-to men for each other—a man you can call for wisdom and support.

I am a better man for my friendship with Joe.

I don't know what I would do without the straight men in my life.

It's hard to believe I was once so afraid of straight men: the enemy. *Enemy* might be too strong, so let's say *potential adversary*. Sure, I had met and befriended exceptions to the rule (rare exceptions, I believed), cool straight men who accepted me for who I was. I knew it was possible.

But as a gay man, I also endured random verbal abuse and witnessed the disgust in straight men's eyes for seeing me as I am. Under the guise of new friendship one straight man invited me to a conversion weekend designed to overcome the "gay curse." So yeah, I owned some shit around straight men. I needed to do my own work.

I didn't know I would do my work with straight men, that they were the *only* ones who could love and heal wounds inside me I vowed I would never, ever let a straight man see. I could *never* expose that vulnerability.

But they saw me.

And they loved me.

In July of 2013, I published my second novel, titled *King Mai*. Takes place on a Midwestern farm. One theme is the friendships between gay and straight men.

I sometimes believe I wrote my first two books exclusively for my New Warrior brothers from MKP. Beneath the plot, the outdoor sex, the kidnapping of baby ducks (not in a sexy way, merely a normal two-men-kidnapping-water-fowl kind of way), beneath all the drama lies the familiar struggle of gold and shadow, and if there's one story both straight and gay warriors love to discuss, it's the struggle of gold and shadow.

On the day I finished writing a first draft of *King Mai*, my buddy Snake happened to stop over at my house. When he rang the bell, I had been writing about the two main characters saying goodbye and as sad as they were, I felt worse. I loved these characters for hundreds of pages and I had to say goodbye, too. I cried while sharing with Snake what this book meant to me.

He listened thoughtfully, eyes focused on me while I described a final scene where Vin Vanbly and Mai Kearns explore the family farm, holding hands.

Snake said, "You should have them tour a barn and look at all the rusted equipment. They recognize those broken tills and old combines might be how farmers show love each to other. Through all those machines they intend to fix one day."

"Yes," I said, eager to reinforce a theme in the book. "It's how straight farmers say, 'I love this guy.'"

"Maybe," Snake said. "Maybe not only straight men. Might be that *all* men love each other through machines and equipment."

Right.

I had assumed something—not particularly negative, but still, assumed—because of an old sore spot in me that used to be jagged and angry. Having deep friendships with straight men is no longer a novelty, but sometimes my old programming surfaces. I will always need straight male friends to point out my basis and blind assumptions.

Vin Vanbly, the narrator of my stories, at one point thinks to himself:

> We're so busy defining ourselves as gay men and straight men, we forget we share a whole word in common. We are men. Despite one rather substantial difference, we should remain curious to see what we learn from each other. What's it like over on your side of manhood? Oh yeah? We don't do anything like that over here. But then again...maybe we do.

Snake earned the right to make plot suggestions because he read my first book, *King Perry*, and after finishing told me, "I loved it. I did. But it definitely confirms I am one-hundred-percent straight. Holy shit did it confirm that."

I would be a different man without Snake in my life.

My life would be less without Joe.

And Harry. And Matt. And Kyle, Chad, Ron, Eric, Kai, Kirt, Mike, Roger, Daniel, Hunter, Kevin, Tim, David, and let me tell you a story about the friendship between me and Brett. Wait, wait...there are too many men to list.

That's why I had to expand the circle to ensure I didn't miss any names. If you flip to the dedication page in *King Mai*, it reads:

To all my MKP brothers, especially the straight ones.

WHERE ARE YOU HEADED, VIN VANBLY?

IT'S ODD, I know.

My first book, *King Perry*, is set in 1999. Narrator Vin Vanbly is thirty-two years old.

The second book, *King Mai*, is set in 1996. Vin is twenty-nine years old.

Between these two full-length novels, I offered three chapters on my website to the reading public from the sixth book (you read that right, sixth) with a new narrator. That book, *King Daniel*, is set in 2013.

A savvy reader might set down the Earl Grey tea, gently remove her/his reading glasses and then politely exclaim, "WTF? Does this idiot author know what he's doing?"

That's debatable.

But there really is a plan.

When I first conceived of writing *The Lost and Founds* as a book series, it was clear to me that readers wouldn't enjoy a repeat of the same story over and over. The first kinging (*King Perry*) is exciting because readers have no idea what's happening. (Well, hopefully.) Is Vin insane? Are these random events leading to something? Why kidnap a duck? It's a little maddening, but that's part of the fun. Uh...right? We had fun, right? (Gulp.)

The second king story must offer new surprises, a different favor of surprise than those offered up in the first book. If Vin's style becomes too predictable, by the third novel, readers will yawn and say, "Oh right, here comes that time of the weekend when they steal something. Right on cue."

Booooo-riiiiing.

I realized that each King Weekend novel had to offer something unique from every other story. New insights about the narrator, Vin, and more revelations of his strange and sad history. Also, the stories themselves had to be unpredictable in some ways. This made me consider that if a reader followed Vin's King Weekends moving *forward* through time, starting with the very first kinging, you'd watch Vin get better and better at this. Better, more polished Vin = more boring.

C'mon. Stories have to have a little random unpredictability, right?

I realized that if the novels occurred three years apart and traveled *backward* in time, you'd catch Vin making more mistakes, more blunders. And gosh...what if one of the kingings from his early days doesn't *take*? What if he fails to king the guy? Wouldn't that be interesting?

Readers need not worry—even looking at his past kingings, Vin remains the same weirdo narrator with word obsessions, food fixations, and the unflappable ability to manipulate the hell out of anyone in a ten-foot radius. (He's still scary like that.) But he's a little less polished. Makes more mistakes. One can only wonder what kind of screw-ups we will see in the third book of this series, the one that takes place in New York City, 1993.

But I also wanted the books to be interesting in any sequence, so a person who reads the books out of order will find odd little mysteries solved along the way. The big secret location in *King Mai* is mentioned in *King Perry* during a paragraph where Vin waxes on about the power of forgiveness. No one would normally catch that detail, but if you read *King Perry* after reading *King Mai*, you will easily notice each time Vin remembers Mai Kearns, who is mentioned liberally in *King Perry*. Read them in sequence or not—either way, you get a few cute little surprises.

Each of the six books are linked to the other five books in numerous ways. Each book has clues about Vin's real name.

Each of the six kings is somehow represented in every other book, either mentioned directly or prophesized, weird little clues dangling like Christmas tree ornaments. There's a single sentence in *King Perry* that reveals the physical locations for books two, three, and four. Secrets about Book Five are scattered throughout *King Mai*.

I love shit like that.

Oh, and then there's the sixth book in the series, the one that takes place in our modern day. By releasing a few chapters between each major novel, readers get to see what's been happening with all the Found Kings in the world. Of course, new mysteries are suggested. What happened to Vin in 2005 that ended his kinging? What state did he fall into requiring his tribe to protect him? Who is D.C., the king present in 2013 who leads in Vin's absence? Have we met that man in one of the published books already?

Mysteries and riddles, riddles and enigmas. Fun, no?

If I were a reader of these strangely told tales, I would threaten the author in my most threatening voice, saying, "You bastard, you better have a plan for all these loose ends. This better tie up better than the television show *Lost*. If there's a sideways world where everyone is already dead, *you're* dead."

In response, I would say, "First of all, quit threatening me. You sound psycho. Secondly, there's a plan."

There's a plan.

While many people loved the had-to-be ending of *King Perry*, still, a few hated it and were upset there was no traditional HEA (Happily Ever After). My books brush against established romance genre tradition. But to my way of thinking, of course Vin doesn't get his big happy in the first book. How interesting would Harry Potter be if he finished off Voldemort in the first book? For six more seven-hundred-plus-page novels we'd read about Harry, Ron, and Hermione getting drunk off butterbeer and playing that irritating game on broomsticks. Bleah.

Can I pull this off? Should I have plotted a more traditional sequence? I guess we'll find out. Even if I eventually decide I probably shouldn't have done this, I honestly believe I won't regret it. These tales are so much fun to write. The unfolding mysteries! The complexities of writing a character three years earlier! The tangled path toward redemption!

So, yes, Vin's got to suffer a bit more. We will learn more about his sad life, the strange, inexplicable events that drew him to the world of kinging. There are a few more bumps ahead for him. But remember in *King Perry*, Vin said, "I'm a sucker for happy endings."

That line? That was a clue.

HAPPY MOON RECESSION BIRTHDAY TO ME

MY OLDER sister, Andrea, likes numbers.

She prefers prime numbers, so the best birthdays are those years when your age is not divisible by any other number except one and itself. She enjoys books about physics, reads articles about string theory, and she often sends me links to quantum theories, anomalies found in the galaxy and beyond. Oddly, she's not into science fiction. Time and space are fascinating enough, making embellishment unnecessary.

Which is not to say she isn't creative. Or inventive. Years ago when I was visiting my family in Illinois, she explained Moon Recession Birthdays and I foolishly believed for a few seconds this was a real thing.

Several years ago, probably 2010, Andrea explained how the moon retreats from the earth by 3.8 centimeters each year (for those of us who slept through the entire world converting to metric, that's roughly 1.5 inches). If you, like me, have grown rather fond of that galactic rock in the sky, this news is alarming. The moon is slipping away. Of course, over your lifetime you won't notice the difference, but Andrea felt we ought to celebrate the moon's proximity by honoring the birthday on which your height equals the distance the moon has retreated from the earth.

When she finished explaining, she excitedly told me, "Your Moon Recession Birthday is the year you're a living yardstick for how far the moon receded." We were eating dinner at our parents' home, so I turned to my other siblings who had already heard Andrea's calculations.

I asked, "Have you guys heard this crazy shit?"

Matt said, "My Moon Recession Birthday is coming up when I turn 47."

My younger sister Eileen pouted. "I missed mine already. It was last year."

I am 5' 9" and that means a total of 69 inches. How many years would it take for the moon to retreat 69 inches? Forty-six years. My Moon Recession Birthday occurred in 2013.

On a business trip last year, I explained the Moon Recession Birthday concept to California coworkers at an intoxicated happy hour. I'm not sure how the Moon Recession Birthday topic came up. I mean, only I could have introduced it (since it's not a thing outside our family) but at the time it seemed relevant to our conversations.

Alcohol makes many stories seem relevant.

My coworkers listened in awe. The ensuing silence meant either deep admiration for my sister's ingenuity or deep dread that our family's lunacy was contagious. Hard to tell. Three work days later I concluded it was the former because these California coworkers built a website called the Moon Recession Birthday Calculator and sent me the link. You type in your height, click the Submit button, and voilà: your Moon Recession Birthday is calculated.

I typed in my height and our preliminary calculations were correct: 2013 was my destined Moon Recession Birthday.

As my birthday approached last August, I struggled with how to celebrate this auspicious occasion.

It was confusing for two reasons. First, this is a completely made-up thing, so there aren't any rules. Should I have instructed friends to buy me moon-related gifts? Was I required to stare at the moon until dawn? I could only assume a round cake with white frosting, right? Secondly, big birthdays freak me out, the significant changeovers. I was never irritated by turning thirty or forty, but the year after those: thirty-one and forty-one. Those years meant, you're *really* in your thirties/forties now. (Of course, Andrea would argue thirty-one and forty-one were excellent prime number years.)

I'm not sure how to spend the significant birthdays. I guess every birthday is significant, especially the older I get.

Aging scares me. I'm worried I'm not strong enough to handle degenerating cartilage in the knees or the disappointments of never being president of the United States. Never becoming a dancer. Never visiting the Amazon rainforests. It's not that I wanted these things in life, but each birthday reminds me certain possibilities will never come to pass.

Don't get me wrong—I *could* book at trip to the rainforests tomorrow, but screw that. Big fucking snakes. That's all I need to hear; the Amazon rainforests are not for me. I generally quite enjoy the life I'm living, thank you, but growing older means receding from youthful potential, those years of unfolding promise. I am a living yardstick to the chubby tot I once was.

One bright summer day when I was a seven or eight, Mom yelled at me from the upstairs landing (possibly about not making my bed again) and I was so enraged I stormed out the front door, trotted down the front steps just like a big boy and marched away from the house. I'd never stormed out like that. Never. I had no idea where to go. I heard the screen door open and bang closed. Andrea immediately fell into a half step behind me, begging to know what was happening. Where was I going? When would I return? Even at that age I recognized the worry in her voice.

"Are you running away?" she asked.

This question sliced through my anger and gave me pause. I hadn't considered running away, but I was sure headed *somewhere*. But where? Did I *want* to run away? I didn't even pack any sandwiches. I paused for these considerations and my anger dialed down. But I had my pride so I kept marching toward a destination unknown.

Andrea walked next to me, jogging half steps to keep up with my furious pace, and she promised me, *promised* if I didn't run away, she would play Monopoly with me. But please, come home. *Come home.*

I stopped. Turned around.

I came home.

At that age, it's not easy to find people willing to play Monopoly.

Though I did not know my true intentions, nevertheless, I labeled the experience When Andrea Stopped Me From Running Away.

A few years later, Andrea headed off to Girl Scout camp for a week and I cried. I bawled my eyes out thinking of her not being in the house for a full week. The night she packed her camping gear, I honestly believed I was a brave little toaster, hiding my feelings, but looking back, my weeping trips to the bathroom for more Kleenex possibly gave me away more than I thought. She came into the bedroom I shared with my younger brother and into the darkness she said, "It's okay. It's only a week. You'll be okay."

She and I are not the same people back When Andrea Stopped Me From Running Away. As adults, we're not close. I grieve that, but I accept it. We see the world differently and those differences create division. Almost a decade ago she confided her belief gay people are a mistake in the world. After we discussed her recently adopted philosophy, I contemplated cutting her out of my life completely. How could I respect myself in relationship with someone whose religious views told me I was a walking mistake?

But she's always my big sister and when I think of running away from her, I remember she kept her promise. We played Monopoly. Relationships are complicated and running away doesn't always provide the desired relief.

This year I celebrated my Moon Recession Birthday the best I could, waving goodbye to the retreating moon and my receding youth. I did my best to remember who I was, who we *both* were, back when I thought I couldn't live without her for one week. We may have grown apart, but we still make each other giggle. I email her cat videos. She sends me physics links.

A year or two ago, my friend Michael arrived at my house for dinner and handed me the day's mail from the mailbox. I had received a package. No return address. We opened it and inside found a small round cake, frosted completely yellow, a blazing sun of a cake. Also included in the box were nine cookies (bubble-wrapped very carefully), each cookie intricately decorated. One was covered with blue and green sprinkles. Another cookie was a murky orange with cream-colored swirls and a red circle in its lower left side. One cookie sported three stripes of orange candy jimmies, carefully applied individually, piece by piece.

Michael said, "What are these supposed to be?"

"Planets," I said, and I knew it was true. "That one is planet Earth and this one is Jupiter with its red eye. This one, the red planet, is Mars. Those candy sprinkles are rings around Saturn."

We used Google Images to confirm the identities of Uranus, Mercury, and Neptune. Michael was incredulous at the intense fidelity between the decorated cookies and the online visual representations of those planets.

"This would have taken hours," he said, amazed. "Who would do this?"

I had known the answer as soon as I saw the blazing sun cake.

I said, "My big sister."

THE FINAL BLESSING

DURING SWEEPS week on any given television drama, you can count on a main character's parent showing up to announce, "I'm dying."

It's funny, because we never hear about that beloved parent before this episode but the main character you've watched for two seasons is suddenly jubilant that "my mom, my best friend," is due to visit. And you can bet that parent is coming either to die or announce a divorce. If it's a death, then there's an inordinate amount of time spent on that parent's final blessing, the last words imparted to their beloved child: a final forgiveness, sage advice, look after your sister, and occasionally (like on the 1980s night-time soap, Falcon Crest), where to find the secret stash of Nazi gold.

I probably watch too much TV, but I must admit that I wondered if my father would have a final blessing for me in his last days. Maybe some sage advice to put our entire relationship in perspective with just a few words. Maybe "look after mom." And hey, maybe he hid a pirate chest's full of jewels and gold somewhere. It could happen.

Still, I thought a dying parent's final blessing was one of those fake television things. A tearjerker for ratings. I didn't realize that it was real and could change your life.

Three days before he drew his final breath, my father's words were sparse and conversations consisted of only a few sentences before he drifted to sleep. One afternoon I tiptoed into the den where we had established his hospital bed.

"Who's there?" he asked in a dreamy, unfocused voice.

I took his hand in mind and stood over him.

"It's me, Edmond."

He said, "Hi, honey."

I got choked up and managed to say, "Hey, Dad."

His hand was exhausted, mostly bones, the skin a weathered treasure map of bruises and scars, indicating a life lived hard. I could no longer tell his work scars from his liver spots from the rapid aging brought about by death from cancer. He faced the wall and I held his hand and watched him breathe.

Then he said, "Edmond. It's been a pleasure."

He drifted away to sleep.

A pleasure?

It's been a *pleasure*?

My heart broke with soft grief, this tender summarization of our life together. I would describe our relationship with many adjectives, some of them flattering and some, well, not. We laughed together quite a bit. We shared books. A few years ago at the end of our phone conversations he started saying, "We love you from down here (Illinois)," and I would reply, "I love you from up here (Minnesota)."

We had beautiful moments, he and I.

But we also owned the matching set of father and son baggage, compounded by my being gay, his not loving that, my leaving the Catholic church, and you know, me being a loudmouth who felt it necessary to call him out on his shit. I'm not proud to admit this, but I've raged at him on the phone.

And yet, his final words to me were, "It's been a pleasure."

Even now, those words thrill me.

Weighing the disappointment I have been as a son, our conflicts over the years, the times (intentional and accidental) when I have hurt him or Mom...and *this* is how he summed it up? Surely, he was disappointed that his big football-player-built son never actually played football, the sport Dad worshiped. My father played football for many years in high school and college.

He broke state-wide records. Brought home championships and earned a college scholarship. In the high school where he taught English and Latin, he coached football for many years. After he retired he continued to study football (well, studied and napped through) every weekend game. *Surely* he felt disappointment I never shared his football love?

If he did, he never showed it. Never once said it to me.

I recall another final blessing, this one on a New Years' Eve afternoon a year before I moved to Minnesota. I coerced him into helping me wallpaper a room. Since Dad was skilled as a carpenter, painter, and all-around Mr. Fix It, I pleaded with him to teach me. Secretly, I had hoped the experience would go much like putting up storm windows when I was a kid, whereby I stood around with a screwdriver, sulking, and he did all the work.

Not so.

He expected me to measure, cut, hang, flatten, and essentially do everything he did. Despite this being completely unfair, nevertheless, I learned his tricks for lining up the pattern and how to seal the edges just so. I discovered a sincere pleasure in working side by side with this taciturn man until he announced he was leaving midway through the final wall, which included a tricky window.

"I should get home," he said.

It was only 4 p.m.

I argued, "We're almost done."

But he was already scrubbing his hands in my bathroom sink, fixated on getting back to Mom. After he left, I crumbled into a chair covered in canvas, literally watching glue dry. Inwardly, I cursed his laziness for quitting before he finished, holiday or no. His big evening plans with Mom included dozing in front of Dick Clark's New Year's Rockin' Eve and possibly awakening to watch that damn ball drop in New York. Couldn't he see how little was left to complete? Didn't he realize I didn't want to cut paper around that last window on my own?

Suddenly it was perfectly clear to me that he *did* know these things.

I sat up straight.

He wanted me to finish on my own.

I do believe Pops attempted to teach his thick-headed son a lesson in self-reliance that day. I marveled at how sneakily he made his exit, how he explained nothing as we hugged goodbye.

With snarky defiance, I decided to prove how misguided his faith in me actually was. Yes, I would finish the job myself, but the disastrous fourth wall would so badly wreck that seamless harmony of the previous three walls visitors to my home would gasp and attempt to mask their horror. Some would meekly inquire, "What happened over there?"

Yes, I would show *him* what could happen by quitting early.

I measured. Measured again. Cut the paper. Applied the glue, grousing and inwardly complaining. Sitcom dads never quit early. They stayed to the bitter end. But somehow, I did it. I finished that fourth wall. Worked around the tricky window. Lined up every damn seam.

It looked great.

I felt great.

His final blessing that day was the message, "You can do this without me."

Today is the last day of May, and truthfully, I feel panic that it ends in roughly twenty minutes. My dad died on May 1st, and in just a few minutes, it will no longer be the month that he died. Too soon it will no longer be the season he died and then the year that he died.

I imagine a future in which someone will ask me, "When did your father pass away?"

My automatic response will be, "Gosh, was that nine years ago or eight?"

I hate it.

I'm not interested in mourning non-stop for the rest of my life, but I'm not quite ready to let him go. Once again, he ducked out before I was finished with him. And once again, on his way out the door, he gifted me an amazing blessing.

Well, I have a final blessing too, Pops.

I can do this life without you. I don't want to, but you prepared me well. Thanks to your excellent fathering and generosity of spirit, I can do this.

Dad, truly, it's been a pleasure.

MOM!

MOM!

Mom called a few months ago to reveal significant news from our small town of Huntley—the post office lady retired. I don't believe any national news media picked up the story (Twitter didn't explode) but it was a big deal for Mom and me.

Ever since I left home for college, I've been writing letters or sending postcards addressed to MOM! or MOM & DAD! I enjoy exclamation marks and you're not supposed to use them in your fiction, so I splurge in personal correspondence. I sometimes addressed things as "HEY PARENTAL UNITS!" accentuated with fat, multi-colored markers and a healthy dose of dolphin stickers.

I like dolphin stickers.

Over the years, my dolphin/markers/all-cap screaming mail attracted the attention of the Huntley post office staff. They had witnessed years and years of MOM! and HEY MANNINGS! packages and grew curious about the sender. Once while visiting Huntley, Mom insisted we go in to the lobby area to meet the post office crew.

When I arrived, Mom said, "This is him. He's the one."

They each shook my hand in a subdued manner. I felt like an odd celebrity.

One woman in her fifties said in an eager voice, "At first we suspected you were a special needs."

I could see by the dirty looks from her coworkers they didn't love that particular half-explained revelation, so the woman who is my mother's friend reluctantly gave the context. "For a while we speculated you were Peggy and Joe's grandson or a godchild. When the markers and stickers didn't seem to, well, *age* over a decade's time, we wondered if maybe you had *special needs*. We wondered if they moved you to a group home in Minnesota. Then your mom told us you were thirty-four and actually had a real job."

I looked at Mom and she smiled wide, chuckling. I remember this moment vividly not because my hometown post office assumed I was mentally challenged. Oddly, that didn't offend me or register as insulting. But I remembered because Mom was proud of me. She was *proud* of her weird son and his sticker/marker fetish.

Growing up in our small town, we always owned a post office box, visiting it daily to grab the mail. Mom and Dad never had mail delivered to their home; the very concept seemed absurd. They socialized at the post office, reconnected with high school classmates, friends of the family, and chatted with neighbors who lived just around the corner. Caught up on news. Discussed town issues. The post office was their Facebook.

While buying stamps for forty years and collecting overly thick MOM! envelopes, my mom and the post office staff became friends, aging many decades together in each other's presence. When my dad died, the post office sent a sympathy card and everyone signed it.

I harbor a fondness for the Huntley post office and the people who show kindness to my mom on a daily basis. I myself don't get to perform many daily kindnesses for her.

I'm the kid who moved out of state. Yes, I chose to live here and most days I do not regret that decision. Still, I miss being close to my siblings and Mom. I am keenly aware my distance limits the kind of relationship I could have with each one. With Dad gone, all four kids metaphorically cling to Mom, insisting she not leave us anytime soon. We're not ready to be orphans.

It's not all hilarious MOM! envelopes and delicious homemade spaghetti. Mom and I have a tricky relationship.

She isn't crazy about parts of my life (i.e. my being gay and leaving Catholicism) and I don't approve of her life either, to be honest. But we love each other and struggle our best to show that great love. We talk books, weather, food, and home repair. We enjoy laughing together and over long phone chats, I sometimes share a few of my adventures, the PG versions. We now talk about Dad pretty regularly and retell stories we both already heard. But we love to tell his stories and we love to listen to each other tell them.

When we feud, look out. We both swing the same furious sword, mine forged to razor sharpness, just like hers. When I calm down after our fights, I always return to a long-ago day when I brought her two handfuls of chestnuts fallen from a neighbor's yard. I suppose I was seven years old.

I asked her, "What are these?"

She said, "I don't know. Let's find out."

We lay on the floor and spread open encyclopedias until we found an answer. I remember marveling Mom could not know things about the world and be so at ease in admitting it. I also thrilled my question was so important it warranted stopping her day to find answers with me. Even though I now suspect she recognized chestnuts and was trying to install the virtue of curiosity in me, I still envy her ability to say, "I don't know" with confidence and grace.

Some days I describe our relationship as tricky.

Other days, it's not tricky at all.

She loves her son.

I love my mom.

A few months ago, Mom said, "Did I tell you the lady at the post office retired?"

Mom sent her a card and a gift certificate to the Olive Garden, thanking her for all her years of devoted service and friendship. Mom explained she'd miss their regular chats and retrieving boxes decorated in colored markers and sparkly stickers addressed to MOM!

In a dry voice, my mother said, "Guess how I signed the card?"

MAY DAY

HI, POPS.

Snowed hard again the other day. Mostly melted by the next day. Can you believe we've suffered through two blizzards in late April? Yeesh. I know how you like your Minnesota weather updates.

Work is good. Clients are clients. Traveling less these days, which is great.

Ready for the big news? In a few days, I'm going to live in New York City. No, really, Dad. I'm staying for a month. I'm working on the third book in a series and it takes place in New York. I'm going to live there during May, in the Chelsea neighborhood. Should be fun. Secretly, I'm terrified.

I want to talk to you about it.

I'm not sure what I'd expect you to say. You'd grunt. Awkwardly assemble some encouraging phrase. You would remind me I succeeded in the past on various adventures and say something like, "You're good at this sort of thing."

I could always tell two things about your affirmations. First, they were always hard and angular for you to say aloud. Over the years I definitely got the impression nobody made much effort to encourage you or explain that you were wonderful. As a parent you stumbled finding the words, words you never heard growing up. Mom used to regularly say you were wonderful, a compliment that made you bashful, but I don't believe anyone encouraged you much as a child.

The second thing I could always tell was how much you meant it, even if the words were unsure. You meant it. You tried hard to show us all your love. It was you, in your fifties, who originated the big hugs, more than pat-on-the-back hugs, squeezing us hard to show us all you loved us *that* much.

I miss you, Pops.

We all do.

We talk about you all the time. Whenever the five of us eat a meal together, we toast you with orange juice, milk, or cocktails, whatever is available. I don't know when you talked to Matt last, but he's dating someone. We all like her a lot. She is funny and smart and they are sweet together. Eileen moved into her new place. She decorated it beautifully. Andrea went to Israel and brought us all water from the Dead Sea. That was cool.

On the phone, Mom and I will often laugh over something ridiculous you said. Not long ago, she retold about a night long before us kids were around when you smoked three dozen cigarettes *at once* as a prelude to quitting smoking. You couldn't bring yourself to throw cigarettes away because they were so expensive. What else would a reasonable person do? You had a friend light all thirty-six at once while you grasped them with both hands like a fat bong and inhaled as much as you could. Mom recalled another time, a long-ago Sunday when you broke the church's new crucifix moments before it was to be blessed by a visiting bishop. The bishop, an old friend of yours, entered the sacristy to find you holding Jesus' broken body in one hand and the cross in the other.

Legend has it he looked at you, shook his head, and said, "Oh, Joe."

You looked at him and said, "He was already crucified when I got here."

Good one, Pops.

Then, Mom and I get quiet and talk about the things we miss. Your voice. Your absurd expressions, especially feigned innocence. Your quiet.

Sometimes I call home when I know Mom isn't around so I can listen to you on voicemail, promising to return my call. We persuaded Mom not to change the outgoing message so we can all hear you from time to time. Your wristwatch alarm hangs from the key rack in the den and still goes off at 1 p.m. every single day. The alarm you never discovered how to disable is now important to us. Whoever is in the house when it starts beeping yells out, "Hi, Dad!"

Mom considers it your daily check in.

Mom's doing good.

She keeps herself busy with church work, volunteering and many house projects. She still works in the yard and washes the kitchen floor on her hands and knees. She hosted Easter brunch for all the families a few weeks ago. She made the egg dishes, ham, salads, and the yummy apricot coffee cake dribbled with frosting and carefully arranged jelly beans. Everyone brought the usual dishes and had fun celebrating. A great party.

Your church friends miss you. They tell stories about you after weekday mass. Mom recently reminded me how, years ago in front of your morning mass group, Father Garrity said, "Joe, tomorrow it's your patron saint's day, St. Joseph the Worker." In your dry voice you said, "He's not *my* patron saint. I follow St. Joseph the Idler." The entire congregation laughed. Aunt Barbara and Mom recently reminisced that hilarious moment and Mom wanted to remind me. Like I would forget.

I know your and Mom's best friends, Clarice and Ed, miss you. They plan things for Mom to do—trips, dinners, prayer groups. They keep her busy.

Remember the last time you were in the hospital, two months before your death? I walked in Sunday morning and to hear you laughing heartily, your face shining. I felt shock because for a second I truly believed you might get better. You looked like your old self. I could hear other laughter as I entered the room and soon saw Ed and Clarice chortling.

I kissed you on the forehead and said, "You look good. You must have had an energizing visit from great friends."

You beamed and said, "I did. But they left. Then Clarice and Ed showed up."

My mouth dropped open.

Ed howled with laughter. You giggled with glee.

I say shit like that sometimes.

Pops, I may have inherited your obnoxiousness.

Hey, want to hear a weird coincidence?

There has been a tickle in the back of my brain for weeks now to send Mom a huge bouquet of flowers on May 1st. It's May Day. Mom used to make May Day baskets with flowers for Grandma and all her friends. Do you remember? Little construction-paper baskets with fragile spring violets and lilies of the valley pulled from our yard. Home-baked treats. Love notes to Grandma's octogenarian friends, reminding them we loved them as part of our family.

May 1st is also the day I arrive in New York City.

I considered sending flowers for Easter but something in me said, "No, wait until May Day."

The flowers would be my way of reassuring Mom while I am in New York. She's nervous about my upcoming trip. The flowers would communicate, "Don't worry about me. I'm going someplace new but you will see me again. In the meantime, I'm having an adventure."

Yesterday I called Mom to update her on the April blizzard (she likes the Minnesota weather updates too) and on the phone, she reminded me May Day is the two-year anniversary of your death.

Well, shit.

I don't know if I blocked the offending day from consciousness or perhaps I genuinely forgot. I have too many thoughts in my head; dates are bound to slip. I dunno. When I realized I forgot you died on May 1st, I immediately got sad, wondering how I could possibly forget the miserable day you left us.

But then I was comforted by the idea maybe I didn't exactly forget. Maybe the strong, insistent notion to send Mom flowers on May Day was actually a subtle communication from you, like the 1 p.m. alarm on your wristwatch.

Maybe you wanted to send a message to Mom, saying, "Don't worry about me. I'm someplace new but you will see me again. In the meantime, I'm having an adventure."

Online I selected huge, gorgeous flowers exploding bright colors, brash and unforgettable. The bouquet was magnificent and ridiculous, just like you. I signed the florist card, "From all of us who love you."

The wording is a little awkward, I know. But it's sincere.

I learned from the best.

THE DANDELION KING

I BELIEVE in ManKind Project's mission of service until it happens to conflict with the time I crawl from bed on Saturday morning. That's when I grumble about "stupid mission stuff." Nevertheless, I dragged myself from sleep and stumbled over to Dan's home early yesterday morning so we could join other barely awake New Warriors to work for Habitat for Humanity. Dan organized about fourteen men to work with Habitat's master gardeners to landscape a home in North Minneapolis. We cleared dead lawn, planted and cedar-chipped dozens of perennials, and left the family with a gorgeous, sculpted front and side yard, matching their neighbors in green, growing beauty.

Well, everyone else did that.

I chose a completely different, fairly useless assignment.

After we first arrived, I stood in the backyard meeting the Somali homeowners. While everyone stood around chatting, one of the master gardeners surveyed the back lawn carpeted with dandelions. She said with obvious disappointment, "We're focusing on the front and side yard today. It's too bad because yellow is the symbol of drought in Somali culture."

Enough said. The yellow drought flowers would be my sole focus for our time onsite.

As volunteers drank coffee, milling around waiting for the Habitat organizers to start giving orders, I noticed a curious phenomenon.

The back curtains in the first-floor windows swooshed open and then zipped close mysteriously, fluttering every few seconds as if by a strong wind inside the house. And yet, I could see no one. Spooky. The phenomenon was easily explained by the father: his curious but extremely shy children. The oldest child was twelve and the remaining six were younger. I amused myself watching the curtains flail open and closed.

A few minutes later, we gathered in the front yard and leaned on rakes to listen to the master gardeners' master plan. As they explained bush placement, the front curtains began their whiplash dance. I decided to investigate. I had already self-assigned myself the role of dandelion picker, so the details of the planning session did not concern me. Instead of listening, I made goofy faces at the living room picture window. I still hadn't seen any children. I crossed my eyes and bared my teeth, I scrunched my nose and then made my eyeballs go completely white. Each new facial tic was met with a screeching chorus as children fled and seconds later scurried back. They showed themselves to me. I taunted them by turning away from the window until one tapped the window, *tic-tic-tic*, then I would flip around, my face contorted in a bizarre new expression.

They screamed and fled; returned and screamed. Tapped on the window, *tic-tic-tic*, and I spun around again. Repeated as necessary.

Then it was time to get to work.

For an hour, I knelt and dug with a skinny two-tonged yard implement which looks like a stretched-out fork. I'm sure the instrument is named, but I'm too lazy to Google the answer. I found myself enjoying this and accumulating a small mountain of dead yellows. I achieved garden nerd satisfaction each time I felt the muffled snap of an underground dandelion root break beneath the soil. Pulling up a root eight inches long would make me shiver with delight. Soon I heard familiar tapping from the back window. *Tic-tic-tic.* The curtains whooshed once again.

I smiled and waved once or twice, but I concentrated on the task at hand.

For the next few minutes a voice muffled behind class would cry out, "Make a funny face!"

"Sorry," I yelled cheerfully. "I have to work now."

"Make a funny face!" they cried.

"Come help me," I yelled back. "Come help."

For the next half hour, we taunted each other until they made tentative steps onto the back porch, then dared to come and stand right next to me while I sweated over the next extraction. The weed pile grew bigger and bigger.

"Wanna help?" I asked, and they giggled and ran away, chattering happily in Somali.

You have never seen such gorgeous children. Seriously, each one more handsome than the next. Only my four stunning cousins ever rivaled that beauty in one set of siblings. (Shout out to Anita, Bithika, Kamala, and Narayan.) Shy and laughing, eager and playful, four of the seven gradually came to say my name aloud before running away: "Ep-mon." (We wore name tags.) The two youngest, twins I presumed, sat on the back steps with their tiny hands on their tiny knees, wide-eyed at all the excitement. One twin would stand up, wobbling, then land on her butt, equally excited as her brothers and sisters.

Finally, the oldest boy said, "We will help."

One thoughtful master gardener from Habitat for Humanity brought several kid-sized trowels and a small shovel, as well as cute work gloves for smaller hands. I gathered them together and tried to give demonstrations on how to extract dandelions by the root.

I said, "The best satisfaction comes from getting out as much root as is possible without damaging the surrounding soil."

Well, that was what I intended to say.

I got as far as "The best satisfaction—" before the four children scattered across the yard to start digging. One ditched his little-kid shovel and instead dragged an adult shovel over fifty dandelions, searching for one to dig out. Two other kids followed suit and found adult-sized hand trowels.

While I watched nervously, they began to attack the lawn.

Nobody stayed for my extraction lesson, but how hard could this be? I can be a control freak sometimes, so I ordered myself to chill out and let the little energy balls go dig. Knock yourselves out, kids.

The first sibling returned with a trowel full of mostly grass and one yellow dandelion resting on top, snapped off not far below the head.

"See?" she said to me shyly.

"Yes, that's good," I said. I lied. She had done a terrible job.

She ran away to dump it in my established pile of drought flowers. Her older brother appeared in front of me as she trotted away.

"Yes?" he said. "See?"

"Yes," I said. "That's right, now try to—"

He ran away to join his sister at the dandelion burial mound.

"This is a big one," challenged his younger brother, beaming.

True enough, he captured a big dandelion. I liked this kid a lot. His chubby cheeks and middle-child status reminded me of me. He grinned big and I felt a kindred spirit.

He said proudly, "It's big!"

"Yes, that's great," I said, "But you have to—"

He smiled this big, happy grin and jerked away. Off to the graveyard for weeds.

The sister returned and presented a harvested dandelion in a *generous* pile dirt.

"Oh," I said, openly alarmed. "You got one, yeah. Careful not to get so much dirt, okay?"

What had I done? I encouraged a gaggle of children to attack the yard. How upset would their father be when he saw the destroyed grass, divots everywhere? I probably shouldn't have encouraged them.

Oldest brother returned to challenge his younger bro. He said, "*This* is a big one."

"Yes," I said a little less generously.

"How about this one?" said the next kid in line. "Big one?"

I said, "Yeah."

"What about this one?"

"Look at mine."

I was no longer happy.

The never-ending parade of energetic Somali children meant one was frequently standing before me demanding praise and now *I* couldn't get work done. So, not only was one side of the yard being gutted open with shovels, but worse yet, *I* wasn't productive myself.

This is where I stall in life. Being a better person, growing my compassion is fine, yes yes, that's good and all. But now I'm at *work*. Or now I'm *busy*. This is the intersection where I drop the ball in relationships. Yes, friend, your feelings are important but Best Buy closes in half an hour and I have two other errands to run. Call you back? I get too focused on productivity. And I'm not being absurd or too hard on myself either. Someone has to mow my lawn, do laundry, renew car tabs, research a better cell phone plan, etc. Daily life takes a lot of effort. I don't always have time for a compassionate "blessed be," spiritually enlightened response.

I daydream my compassion or big-heartedness will be needed while I'm hosting the Oscars. Or when I happen to pass a burning orphanage and *someone* must rescue Skittles, the beloved cat trapped upstairs. Yes, the Big Shining Moments. (Although honestly...Skittles would be shit out of luck, because I get easily confused about directions, especially when I'm trapped in a burning building with a terrified, scratch-happy cat. I don't foresee a great outcome for Skittles in this scenario.)

Maybe I'm not ready for the Big Shining Moments. I have to keep practicing on the small ones. I find small moments available daily, the chance to be a king in someone's life. A king.

I know when these opportunities present themselves because they often conflict with my productivity. Whenever I wait for the Big Shining Moments, I forget it might be happening right now.

On my knees in this stranger's yard, I had to choose the greater importance: pluck dandelions *the right way* or accept these young gardeners presenting their finest work?

I decided to become the Dandelion King.

"This is a big one, isn't it?" said the eldest, eyes beaming.

"It's incredible," I said. "You're awesome!"

He bolted.

"I did this one myself!" his sister shouted. "I did it."

"You're doing beautifully," I said with enthusiasm.

Their father entered the backyard and after watching the children parade to Ep-mon-d (they had improved significantly), he laughed and started weeding himself. His children ran to him and softly cried, "Aabee, Aabee!" ("Father, Father!") He would dig out a dandelion, placing it upon their shovel and the kid would carry it to me for approval before dropping it on the weed pile.

"You are wonderful," I sometimes said and I hoped they understood the praise was not about the weed itself..

After seeing the excitement in her brothers and sisters, one of the two very young twins watching from the porch cautiously joined in. She walked to me very carefully, very slowly, balancing a plastic, child's trowel of brown dirt, lacking any greens, weeds, or yellow dandelions whatsoever. Just a pile of dirt. She managed to remain upright, an accomplishment in itself.

She stood before me with her eyes on me expectantly. Too young to speak, there was nothing she could say.

We blinked at each other a moment and I said, "You are the most wonderful dandelion picker!"

She nodded before she turned and walked to the weed pile. Or maybe she drooped her head because a hand-trowel full of dirt is pretty heavy for a toddler. I prefer to believe she understood exactly what I said and she acknowledged me.

After all, who doesn't want a blessing from the Dandelion King?

DEARLY BELOVED

HAVING BEEN born during the Martin Luther King riots in 1967, I was roughly a hundred years too late to go to a Charles Dickens' wedding. I read a lot of Dickens in my teenage years ("a lot" as in all of them) and the endings often boasted the most delightful highbrow weddings. In envisioning these massive wedding receptions, a reader assumed they served amazing wedding cake, right? Something massive, five tiers, thick white frosting. If invited to a Victorian wedding party for a Dickens' aristocrat, hell yeah, I'd go.

When non-aristocratic characters tied the knot in a Dickens' novel, the beloved Miss Skiffins to Mr. Wemmeck (*Great Expectations*) and Bella Wilfer to her true love, John Harmon (*Our Mutual Friend*), you couldn't always count on actually getting a piece of wedding cake.

Oh, their weddings definitely included cakes: jelly rolls, half-frosted, sideways cakes, strange constructions baked by well-meaning simpletons who did not understand the difference between flour and sugar. Dickens described Victorian confections that didn't always translate into modern desserts, but I drooled over them anyway. But these weddings suffered more shenanigans, like the jelly roll toppling from the table and the closest toddler eating it using both paws. When discovered, he blinks at the wedding party in wide-eyed astonishment.

These lowbrow weddings boasted quirky artistic spaces, mismatching twinkling lights adorning a boarded-in yard, home-baked treats, succulent roasted meats, random candlelight, and everyone in love with everyone else. Children are serious and adults laugh like children. Inevitably, some delightful minor Dickens' character gets tipsy and confesses his love for another minor character whom you yourself had also come to love.

If a raucous wedding hosted by the Micawbers conflicted with Lucie Manette's swan-studded afternoon tea wedding, I might have to send Ms. Manette my deepest regrets and most sincere congratulations for scoring a French nobleman. Who cares he's disgraced and penniless? You got a title, girl! But I'm sorry, the Micawber wedding would be more hilarious, even if I didn't get any cake.

This weekend, I attended my very first Dickens' wedding.

On October 27th, Meg and Austin married each other in a lumberjack-themed wedding in northern Minnesota. My goddaughters played the adorable roles of Paul Bunyan and Babe the Blue Ox. Everyone wrapped themselves in knit afghans (courtesy of the bride and groom) and witnessed Meg and Austin share their love on the rocky shore of Lake Superior.

I ministered the service.

The day Meg called to invite me to marry them, she cried hard and I cried too, because I love being loved. We laughed, cried more. She is a queen who inspires my heart with her optimism, pragmatism, and her every artistic creation becomes infused with hand-loved, good cheer. Love swirls around her way other women wear perfume. Her father died recently and even in her raw grief for him she exudes this great love. She is not immune from life's hardships and undoubtedly has difficult days, but she chooses to respond to life by cheering it.

Austin is also a Dickens' escapee from the Victorian era. He sports a tangled, fire-red, sea captain's beard which, we discovered several weeks ago at breakfast, can hide up to seven full-sized crayons. (My younger goddaughter initiated this experiment while the rest of us tried to make Austin laugh, making snarky observations over bacon. Austin kept offering greater access to his lush beard, occasionally blinking wide-eyed in ticklish surprise.)

The first time I met him many years ago, I found myself struck by the everyday uniqueness of him. I had never seen such gentlemanly politeness married to casual informality and when he revealed his email included the mashed words, *fascinatedbydinosaurs,* I wondered, "Who the hell is this king?"

They wanted the service short, because they invited family and friends to stand with them on giant rocks overlooking Lake Superior. October temperatures seemed likely to drop into the high 40s. Or 30s. Probably not the 20s, no probably not. But maybe. More likely was a surprise blizzard. And then what would we do with Meg's grandmother?

Meg and Austin both felt iffy on the traditional line stating, "I now pronounce you man and wife," and in the end, they kept deferring to me, telling me to say whatever felt right. While planning their wedding the three of us found it amusing to consider we three are an Iowan, an Illinoisan, and a Wisconsinite organizing a lumberjack wedding in the heart of Minnesota's north shore, Grand Marais. We gossiped about how we love being Minnesotans, even if we are adopted.

The afternoon of the wedding, everyone draped afghans over winter coats, afghans colored red, orange, purple, rainbow colors, and more, colorful protection against Lake Superior's blustery winds. We followed Paul Bunyan (sporting an adorable black felt beard) and Babe the Blue Ox (Meg sewed together a fuzzy blue costume) out to the sun-dappled rocky shoreline. Forgoing rose petals, Paul Bunyan and Babe spread bio-degradable cocoa chips. (In the brief lull before the wedding, we each took turns deeply inhaling the cocoa basket while attempting to convince the Blue Ox not to taste them.)

Meg and Austin trailed behind those Minnesota legends, Meg wearing her home-sewn dress, adorned with cut-out felt shapes—birds, hearts, and a variety of colorful autumn leaves— and thick words she sewed into the fabric, artful expressions of joy and love. Austin wore a spiffy, old-fashioned suit making him look very European, perhaps a German college professor named Fitzroy. He sported a jaunty fedora perched squarely in front. Whenever Austin beamed in our direction, we all raced in to hug him.

I followed wearing my army camos from a surplus store, a red dress shirt and tie under a flannel jacket, bearing my favorite well-worn axe from my garage. Several wedding attendees questioned the necessity of bringing an axe to a wedding and they found no comfort in my saying, "It's a necessary part of the ceremony." After a few uncomfortable glances tossed my way I began to question my wisdom. What kind of minister brings a sharp axe to the ceremony? Probably shouldn't have done that.

Meg and Austin found their spot on a giant sun-soaked rock, the one that felt perfect.

Any lingering skeptics at last understood why Meg and Austin had picked this miraculous setting for their wedding. After a mostly cloudy morning, the sun now beamed madly on the shoreline rocks, reflecting the joyful, hard light right into our faces. We stayed dry but nearby rocks got blasted over and over by dramatic, colossal waves crashing against them. I felt like we stood on black, sparkling coal while cold waves relentlessly chiseled the stone, shaping the day into diamonds.

Some do not appreciate Minnesota's starkness, its raw beauty. They cannot feel the sheer power in a land so cold, do not rejoice in woodsy survival, and don't understand how we might actually crave winter nights spent by firelight. Hey, I'm not all poetry and kitteny about Florida in July, so I do not expect everyone to share this unique flavor of Minnesota love. But please know that it exists. We of the frozen land and many lakes feel it.

Even out-of-state wedding guests felt it that day, too. All of us stood around and gaped, many wrapped in afghans, understanding this rare beauty, the blessing of a late autumn day. Gift bags provided by Austin and Meg supplied hand warmers, knit caps, and local fudge. Nobody suffered standing out on the rocks.

The reception?

Well, think quirky artistic spaces, mismatching twinkling lights adorning a boarded-in yard, home-baked treats, random candlelight, and everyone in love with everyone else. Apple cheddar pie, grasshopper mint pie, blueberry pie, a flourless chocolate cake. A red velvet cake and many different cheeses. Tender strips of pink-hued steak, hot from the outdoor grills. Oh, the succulent smells of roasting meat! The perfect Dickens reception. And we all got cake.

My new friend Noah and I shared a glass of rum punch while his daughters raced by waving their glow sticks. My friend Heather and I bantered playfully with John, recently moved back from Switzerland. I chatted with Libby and Brenda from San Francisco, and they expressed their surprised delight to party *outside* on this northern Minnesota night. Temperatures were in the high 30s, but the ruddy pleasure of warming oneself around a hearty fire while gazing at thousands of stars kept most people outside.

We drank, laughed, and took turns exploring the knick-knack filled house rented for the party, a combination art gallery with old curiosity shop. Three backyard fire pits offered easy opportunity to mingle and make new friends while laughing, toasting, discussing the beauty of this glorious day and gossiping about how much we love Meg and Austin together.

Earlier that day during the wedding ceremony closing remarks, I lifted the axe and said loudly, "Long before horror movies, the axe was used to create and sustain life. Up here in northern Minnesota, they chopped down trees and made homes for themselves. Split firewood, necessary to survive the long winter. With no axe, there was no way to build your life. A sharp axe symbolizes the intention to build a life through hard work and nights nuzzling by fire light. So, by the power of the

Universal Life Church, Hennepin County, and this big, ol' axe, I now pronounce you Minnesotans."

Everyone cheered and waved their colored afghans.

Lake Superior waves crashed the shore, a cymbal explosion of approval.

Meg and Austin kissed.

It was my first Dickens' wedding.

MERRY STICK-MAS

I STOPPED at the closest Kowalski's Grocery to grab my favorite salsa. I intended to edit quite a bit that afternoon and, really, editing goes best with chips and salsa. It always does.

As I approached the store front, I witnessed two parents patiently arguing with their kid, maybe four or five years old. In both hands he firmly grasped a fairly unremarkable walking stick, something he had obviously acquired on their stroll to the store. Based on how they were bundled, this family had definitely walked to Kowalski's.

It was a balmy 40 degrees Fahrenheit in Minneapolis that Sunday afternoon and with the sun grinning hard, well, to Minnesotans, this practically counted as a summer day. Driving to the grocery, I passed hordes of joggers, parents pushing strollers, and hell, I think I saw a woman doing yard work. I do love how Minnesotans greet the December sun as a sign to go play. They say, "Fuck chores. I'm going rollerblading."

Dad tried to coax the stick from his son's hands, *promising* they would emerge and find the stick standing against the brick wall by the bike rack.

I heard the father say, "No one will take it."

While his son said nothing, the pout and mistrust on his face revealed his lack of faith in Dad's words.

The stick! This stick is everything!

You'd guess I spent ten minutes observing this drama but all this occurred during the twenty seconds it took me to approach and pass this family, entering the store. I admitted the fleeting thought, *Oh, let him carry his stick inside.* But when I saw the carefully piled apples, precariously stacked lemon curd jars, and mounds of Christmas candy ready to topple, I realized the parents' wisdom.

Stick disaster lurked in every aisle.

As I searched for my salsa, I reflected about the time in my life when a treasure like a good stick was everything.

I once owned a small cedar chest, a cheap souvenir from when we visited Mt. Rushmore on family vacation. Over the years, I collected a dyed blue feather, two unique pennies, the back of a Cub Scout pin which had broken off something meaningful. I think I remember a piece of colorful string I intended to use for future inventions. A shiny fake gem. Yes, I once owned treasures.

In the grove across from our childhood home, I would find amazing sticks and always relished my good fortune. Holding one in my young hands, I would marvel at how the stick was so straight, so powerful! Not a single knot or irregularity! Only the luckiest boy in the world could find a stick so perfect. I could use it for ninja fighting or when I played pirates with other neighborhood kids.

"Where did you get it?" I imagined other kids would ask with ill-concealed jealousy.

"Oh this?" I would reply casually, twirling the stick over my head and catching it with ease. "I found it."

When I purchased my salsa and left Kowalski's moments later, I saw the stick propped against the brick exterior. The dad had won. At that very moment inside the store, their son fretted anxiously someone might *steal* the one treasure he owned in the world, the one possession he could say was truly his.

I got in my car, strapped myself in. Thought about my writing day ahead and reflected how much I loved salsa. Wondered if I should have gotten cheese to melt over the chips.

I also considered how lucky I was to skip Christmas shopping, a mere two weeks before the holiday. I had decided to remain in Minnesota this year, the first time ever, and while I would miss my Huntley family, I needed a break from constant work travel. Ann, my best friend, would visit from North Carolina. We would stay awake late gossiping and sharing sad stories. We would eat amazing food.

My many Minnesota friends were eager to celebrate with Ann, so with these friends we would create blazing fires in my fireplace, laugh until we couldn't breathe, and become friends all over again. I would attempt to force everyone to drink egg nog, though most people I know hate it. Their disgust would not stop me from trying.

I still have treasures in my life.

I hopped from my car and approached the stick.

I carefully positioned four quarters around the base of the stick, arranged in a pattern so the boy would know a stranger didn't accidentally drop these coins. No, the boy is right—the stick is truly blessed.

I remember a time in my life when a quarter meant riches.

And *four quarters?*

Well, that was like Christmas.

PRIDE SCHMIDE

ANOTHER GAY pride weekend draws to a close and I find myself thinking, "Missed another one." Well, I can't honestly say I *missed* it.

When I first came out of the closet twenty-five years ago, I gleefully attended the big parades, wowed by all the drag queens, leather guys and the entire spectrum between and beyond. I drank cheap beer (with pride) under a nasty parking lot tent smelling of mold and I danced my ass off with glowy things around my neck (with pride). Back when I lived in Chicago, one year I marched down Halsted Street with the Northern Illinois University's Gay Lesbian Union celebrating rural farmland homos, passing out raw vegetables, chanting, "Corn-fed boys, milk-strong girls!"

So, you know, I prided.

But today I mowed the lawn with my crappy, sputtering lawnmower and bagged my trimmings. I spent time wondering how many more summers this junky old mower would last. Then, I did laundry. Bought much-needed sneakers. I considered attending the post-parade festivities, but instead I spent my afternoon with the Geek Squad working out my computer pride.

As the day unfolded I realized I would not attend a single gay pride activity but I didn't mind. The concept of gay pride doesn't exactly appeal anymore.

As I understand it, the pride in gay pride is pride in *survival*. I made it. Fuck you, world, you tried to crush me and here I am, with a feather boa or my big macho boots or perhaps my—I dunno—cyber-Goth piercings and women's lingerie. I do like the idea of celebrating survival, because despite progress made socially and legally, we've witnessed enough gay teenage suicides in recent years to know the world can shit all over queer youth.

But the word *pride* seems almost arrogant to me these days, and that "fuck you, world" attitude doesn't help. It's no longer us against them. It's us against *us*. The world we live in seems to grow smaller, our global community, and if we don't figure out how to love and accept each other, well, we all know how this turns out for humanity—we've all seen *Planet of the Apes*. Make no mistake, those chimps are biding their time, chatting in Yahoo groups about the imminent takeover.

I had gay pride for many years but now it feels outdated, for me at least. Instead of gay pride, how about gay gratitude?

I am grateful to have survived my lonely teenage years. After coming out of the closet, I did not merely survive, but openly thrived, in college, in love, in the family of choice I crafted for myself and those who have adopted me. My experience of love in this world continues to expand to this very day.

But in this banquet of good fortune I never did it on my own, not once, so I'm not sure *pride* is the best word.

At least ten years after I came out of the closet, my beloved older sister explained how some Catholic writers professed it *acceptable* to love me, because gays were a bruise in the flesh that is humanity. This bruise was caused by America's surplus of weak fathers and overbearing mothers, which meant it wasn't my fault I preferred reading Charles Dickens to playing football. The exciting news for me was that God-fearing Catholics could go ahead and love a bruise.

I was stunned, then furious. The conversation crushed me.

She felt amazement I "took it the wrong way," because the entire point was bruises can be *healed*, which meant God could heal my homosexuality and make me healthy again. Normal.

We did not speak for over a year.

It was not gay pride that healed me.

Powerful healing did allow love to flow between my sister and me again and move beyond the bruise conversation. That loving healing was facilitated by a straight man during a group session one Saturday morning in his basement. During my work, I wept in the arms of another man, also straight. Around me in a semi-circle stood men and women, gay and straight. These people didn't have any special healing powers for gays, their only giftedness was they knew me as a man and they loved me.

They *loved* me.

They opened their hearts and dared me to open mine, to let them witness deep, vulnerable grief pour through me. Even while I sobbed, bawling over my childhood role model telling me I was a blight on humanity, I remember worrying a new friend in this semi-circle, a gorgeous Indian woman, would somehow judge my outburst with disgust. I liked her but we were still becoming friends. Who likes to weep in front of a person you do not know well?

When I could finally see through my tears, I found her hand on mine and her soft brown eyes staring into my face. Without a word she communicated she really, *really* loved me.

Leading up to that miraculous healing one Saturday morning, how many nights did my best friend Ann comfort me over the phone? How many times did Heather, the woman who invited me to be godfather to her daughters, tell me softly, "You're part of *our* family now."

Tonight on my back porch, basking in the glow of twinkling gazebo lights and inhaling the scent of freshly cut grass, I will celebrate my own gay gratitude. I give thanks for those who loved me in spite of being gay, for those who loved me because I'm gay, and for those who don't really give a shit I'm gay, they simply love me because, what the hell, they believe Edmond Manning is worth loving.

I am grateful for Stonewall queens, for my friend Ankha who led a radical gay group in the 70s, a group forced to conduct secret meetings. I am grateful for 1980s AIDS activists, and equality activists in the 90s who realized we already knew many, many straight allies. They recognized the "we" in gay pride needed to be more inclusive. And thank you, Jebus, for those gay marriage advocates. We needed every one of them and still do. We have not yet achieved true equality.

For my gay friends who believe in and love the big gay pride weekend, go for it. I hope you wore your shortest shorts to the parade, marched for Rainbow Families, and what the hell, made out with a hot stranger behind the porta potties by The Saloon. (Ahem...not that I ever did that in 1996.) I am grateful for the big gay parade for those years when it spoke to me, and reminded me I had survived.

I'd like to remind my straight friends two important things. First, I love you. You saved me. Secondly, you know you're supposed to buy gay people a gift on gay pride weekend, right? Something big. Like a lawnmower.

Preferably the Black and Decker MM1800 Electric Rear Bag Mulching Mower.

A TRUE NEW YORKER

I HAVE warned family and friends that for the next six months, most of my stories will begin, "Back when I lived in New York..." Their job is to resist rolling their eyes, bite their lower lip, and live with it. Seriously.

Nobody gets to say, "Jesus, Manning, you only lived there a *month.*"

Look, I slept on a mattress on the floor and I am not a young man. I tolerated nightly garbage stacked high in the streets, shocking new urine odor distinctions I never knew existed, and a neighbor who hacked his lungs into a cereal bowl every single morning. I decided he ate his lungs for dinner at night because every morning he did it again: coughed up painful, brown chunks on the other side of our shared bathroom wall. I could hear it from my mattress.

I earned these story rights.

But as many stories as I could tell, the reality is, I was never a true New Yorker.

Oh, I had the New York experience. I explored the city daily via subway. I gave directions to tourists. When a car almost hit me in the cross walk one Tuesday, I pounded a fist on its hood and yelled, "What the fuck?" I jerked my free hand at the WALK icon and screamed, "Watch the goddamn signs!"

Still, that didn't make me a real New Yorker.

Read a book in Central Park.

Partied in Tribeca.

Partied at a street festival in the Meatpacking District.

Laid in trash bags somewhere on 7th Avenue. (The drinking and trash bag incidents are not connected.)

During my month stay, my sophomore year college roommate, Aris, came to town with his wife and kid. He and his business partner were taking public the company he co-founded many years ago. Aris began his morning ringing the start bell on the New York Stock Exchange, and ended celebrating in a high-end Chelsea eatery, the kind where the chef prepares duck-flavored appetizers the size of a crouton.

Despite being twenty-five years older than when we ordered deep dish pizza and watched *Twilight Zone* marathons, we still giggled like teenagers over our naiveté for fancy dinner etiquette. His beautiful wife was a thoughtful conversationalist and great fun. Their kid was quirky and interesting, eager to show me the cool technology in his robot camera.

New York City blessed Aris' big dreams. We toasted and laughed at how our lives turned out. (I didn't want to brag and undermine his big day, but during the month I lived in New York, I myself picked up a few bucks on Wall Street.)

I attended Broadway musicals.

Slogged through an ordinary downpour and grinned madly at all the other soaked Penn Station subway patrons who dared to grin back.

Found the best chocolate chip cookie in all of New York.

None of it made me a New Yorker.

In preparation for my trip, I read a book of beautiful essays by Colson Whitehead. He wrote, "Knowing facts about New York does not make you a New Yorker." He gently argues only realizing the city goes on without you makes you a true citizen. You're a New Yorker when you walk a neighborhood and reflect on how everything changed from when you first saw it.... *That* used to be a coin-operated laundromat. *That* used to be a bodega owned by the friend of a friend of your parents. Now, it's a Duane Reade pharmacy.

I find the idea beautiful, the soft insight that New Yorkers remain for the long haul. Short-timers like me can show up and love the city, sure, but New Yorkers are in it to win. This ever-evolving landscape is their home, and they feel about it the way we Midwesterners feel about our comfy recliners or grilling backyard steaks before sunset on Sunday.

I'm sure others would argue with Whitehead's definition. Don't ask for an easy resolution to "Who is a true New Yorker" because New York doesn't give a shit about answering your questions.

One Sunday near midnight I strolled around Midtown, irritated all the doughnut shops were closed. I thought this was the city that never slept? A nearby show lounge had apparently emptied out, maybe a glam-o-rama type thing because in the course of a few minutes, thirty gaudily decorated, flamboyant gay men and shrill women paraded by me on the sidewalk, laughing, screaming, giving me dirty looks.

One young guy strode alone, staring at eternity, eyes frozen forward. This wasn't a casual glance at the block ahead, he focused a military glare reserved for a dictator's national flag. His hair was coiffed into a 1950s pompadour, tons of product. Glitter gold eye shadow (and matching lashes), ascot, leather jacket and screaming across his chest, a gleaming gold-plated gun, a recognizable Colt 45.

I marveled at his bragging gold firearm, drag-queen eye shadow and bizarre Glamor Guy identity. Was this look something exotic he threw together the way one experiments in New York? Next week would he sport thick-rimmed glasses and cardigans?

Or was this *real* him, the true identity he self-accepted at age twelve? Perhaps he grew up in Idaho and impatiently waited to reach the physical age where he could move to the one city where he knew he'd find acceptance. Maybe he spent his whole life surrounded by people who didn't get him and now, *now* he was home.

Which was true for Gay Glamor Guy?

Never found out. New York does not offer answers.

Some nights I lay flat on my mattress eating chocolate Oreos, staring at the skyline through my apartment's only window. I could always see the Empire State Building's shining spire, a brilliant, glowing beacon boasting architectural achievement and grace. I would reflect how amazing it felt to witness this day, the one now closing, in which millions of people agreed to share the same physical space and act decent to each other. They politely maneuvered around each other. Waited in line behind each other. Sometimes smiled at each other's dogs. Maybe shared a cab.

New York is amazing.

Seriously, where else can you find millions of humans hell-bent on being uniquely themselves while simultaneously agreeing to the invisible rules around entering a subway turn style and navigating a crowded sidewalk? Millions (think about that number—*millions*) of people agree to the most basic kindnesses with each other, all done without discussion. It's just what they *do* every single day. Sure, they fight. They can act terrible. Several gay man were murdered during the month I visited, victims of hate crimes. I'm not denying homelessness and sewage and rats. That's true, too.

New York doesn't mind contradictions.

But if you are desperate for hope in humanity, spend a Tuesday in New York. A Thursday works. (Monday in a pinch.) Every single day New York experiments with a concept called *civilization*. They walk right past each other, not exactly interacting, but not exactly ignoring either. For millions, the flavor of this special love says, "Go live your life, Gay Glamor Guy, or whoever you are at this moment. And I'll go live mine." Make no mistake, it's not convenience or mutual non-aggression, it's love. It could only be love.

If New York is possible, then humanity can do fucking *anything*.

On my last night in town, I caroused from club to club with a friend I made, a real New Yorker. I know he was a *true* New Yorker because within six seconds of our leaving the first bar, he spotted a fat rat hustling across the street. Inside the bar, I had been complaining of my desire to spot a rat. I had been searching for a full month, even hunting for rats in alleys after dark.

As we left the bar he said in a bored voice, "Rat. Right there. We should go to that corner over there. We could get a taxi easier from 8th Street."

The rat scurried into the meaty darkness and disappeared.

Twelve minutes later, after a cab ride spent in hilarious cabbie political banter, we found ourselves a block from our drunken destination. We tipped our driver well and ambled down the sidewalks. Suddenly, my friend lifted his head and screamed. "EDMOND MANNING, EDMOND MANNING, EDMOND, MANNING."

I felt mild embarrassment and asked why he did that. He threw his arm around my neck and said, "Has anyone screamed your name in New York? Anyone screamed it three times?"

"No," I said.

He said, "You've never really lived in New York until your name has been screamed three times in the city."

When he wasn't making indie films, this friend worked as a Central Park tour guide and once admitted he sometimes embellished stories for tourists. So perhaps he fed me a line. I did not care. I wanted to believe it was true, so I did.

I yelled my name aloud, right then, letting my voice hang in the inky night next to his, like shirts on a clothesline.

"No, no," he said, scoffing. "You can't do it *yourself*. It doesn't mean anything unless someone else yells it."

See? Even after a month, I still didn't understand New York.

I may never be a true New Yorker, but now the city has my name.

MONSTERS

WHEN ORDERING a life-sized zombie torso from the Sky Mall catalog, you have no idea whether the reality will match your expectations. Will the glassy eyes appear undead? Do the blackened teeth look rotting enough? Everything looks better in a catalog. Of course, one might inquire as to why an individual *wants* yard art representing a decomposing corpse head and grasping arms.

I wouldn't know.

I don't want that creepy fucking thing in my yard, that's for sure. I purchased the garden zombie as a gift for my friend Ron. He had re-landscaped his back yard that summer and I wanted to help redecorate.

Over our years of friendship, Ron taught me how to cook savory vegetables and duplicate his perfect homemade pesto. He makes cauliflower taste better than candy and his bruschetta can bring tears to my eyes. He's quiet and thoughtful. Around him, I feel calmer. I take deeper breaths. Despite his mild-mannered banker exterior, he's goofy and angular, regularly in touch with his mischievous inner child. For two Halloweens, he transformed his own flesh into the living dead, Zombie Banker, believable enough I refused to stand near him. He knew I hated zombies. Last year, Ron improved on the original undead costume, creating gaping flesh divots on his face and neck that oozed blood whenever he squeezed the flaps, like a zit.

To this day, when friends ask me about my other friends, they say, "So, how's Zombie Ron? What's he up to these days?"

My Sky Mall zombie arrived and I must admit to being impressed. Truly, it embodied every undead quality you could want in a realistic sculpture: writhing in agony, furious, hungry. I waited until Ron traveled on a business trip and snuck into his back yard to position his new garden zombie tastefully amid the shrubs, trying several positions before finding the exact right spot, the right angle. I left the undead in view from the patio doors so his gaze might fall upon it while he chopped kale or broccoli.

He admitted to discovering it while chopping vegetables, confused at first by the unrecognizable lump in the dark and then properly horrified when he realized what it was. He discovered he did not mind dressing as a zombie for Halloween but a decaying corpse in his backyard went too far. He could not love this garden zombie. He tried ignoring it but that didn't work. His eyes were drawn to it every few minutes to make sure it kept its distance. Within 48 hours he threw a tarp over it and carried it into the garage. But then he feared going to his car.

A month later, one chilled Saturday in September, I joined for an outdoor fire. He whipped together his amazing pesto, chopped multi-colored cherry tomatoes and mixed a garlic-infused goat cheese spread to enjoy on bread toasted over the fire.

In honor of my visit, he pulled the garden zombie out of banishment and artistically arranged the corpse in a flower bed near the fire so it was front lit, half in shadows while flickers of flame reflected in the glossy dead eyes. Ron sprinkled dirt over it for that fresh-from-the-grave authenticity. Ron is a good friend.

We toasted the garden zombie, our friendship, and this perfect Minnesota evening. We argued whether the big fat star in our line of vision was the North Star or Mars, both of us too busy enjoying the night and our argument to Google the answer. We sipped wine, told stories, complained about various airports, and in the golden blaze of fire, loved each other as two friends can do.

I told him when I die, as my consciousness twinkles out of existence, I would not mind if this night, this moment, is what flashes through me: sitting under the stars, wrapped in a flannel jacket chuckling with a friend, the cozy glow of a zombie a safe distance away. I could live happily (or rather die happy) with those last impressions fading from my brain.

Later in the evening, our talk grew serious and I shared a disquieting experience from recent work travels. I had been teaching a four-day class to federal law enforcement officers in a southern state. I enjoyed it. The men were funny, respectful, and once they got to know me, they played along with my off-kilter sense of humor. On the last day during a break, a few officers recounted stories of recruits who did not do well at this particular academy. After discussing three men who got drunk and skinny-dipped, the conversation turned toward "gays among us." The tenor of the conversation was not particularly welcoming.

I bristled, thinking, "Please don't anyone say something dickish." Discussing a colleague in training, one man said, "We should have shown that gay guy a real southern welcome: swinging from a tree at the end of a rope."

Eight or nine federal officers actively participated in the conversation up to that moment and another three or four were present in the room. After he said it, nobody said a word in response. A full moment later, a new topic was introduced.

On the plus side, nobody said, "Yeah, we should kill them all!" On the downside, nobody said, "It's inappropriate to suggest murdering gays."

These were federal law enforcement officers, representing a number of different agencies. These folks are trained to protect lives. But maybe not gay lives.

I was so shocked by the statement and ensuing silence I myself did not speak up. I left the room and tried to get calm. Should I have chided them all? Outed myself? Lectured them on their hurtful silence? I was their guest so I had to consider the organization I represented. I struggled with these questions and wondered about my own silence. Mostly I wandered the hallway in shock. It never dawned on me I was surrounded by people who potentially hated me enough to want me murdered. I probably should have said something. Would I later regret my silence? Was I shirking my responsibility to advance gay rights by not turning this into a teachable moment? I probably should have said something.

I had a hard time reconciling his rope-swinging suggestion with my perfect Saturday night in Ron's backyard. Are Ron and I *monsters*? Two middle-aged gay men talking about camping, childhood pranks, family members we love and miss...arguing over stars in the sky...we're so dangerous to civilization we need to swing from a tree at the end of a rope? We were too lazy to Google the North Star. How much value could we provide to an impending gay revolution?

It would be easy to paint that particular officer and those who said nothing as the enemy. They're not. I spent almost a week with these folks. They were goofy and hilarious. We laughed together quite a bit. Even when they were bored with the content they did their best to participate in class to show me respect. The last day I spent with them, a mere four hours after the comment was made, they presented me with a cake they had purchased and decorated, incorporating several week-long jokes. (One of their peers confessed a terror of clowns, so of course, the cake was decorated with plastic clown heads.) They thanked me for coming and cheerfully clapped for me.

Some of them will probably selflessly die protecting civilians. And yet.

As I sliced through the frosting, I couldn't help but reflect on the swinging from a tree comment. Really? Would you murder me? Or if someone else got overzealous and produced rope, would you stand by and let it happen?

Ron and I reflected on the story I shared as we drained the pinot noir and steadily munched the bruschetta. Such tender tomatoes, soaked in garlic and drizzled with olive oil. The smoky taste of the bread cooked over flames tasted like autumn. We discussed the nature of hate and love, how fear grows, and what it takes to change ourselves and the world. We discussed how it feels when strangers, and even family members, consider us freakish for being gay.

If you don't think like I do, you're deluded. If you're too conservative politically, you hate people. If you are too liberal, you're trying to bring about Armageddon. Those with religion consider those without to be monsters. And I admit, I fret over religious zealots with the same fear I reserve for zombies.

I guess we're all monsters to someone.

CREEPY MONKEY

I FOUND a plastic chimp in the cupboard above the stove.

He's smallish (key-chain sized), crouched forward with wide, glassy eyes. I found this chimp grinning in front of my cookbooks and thought, "Hey. A chimp."

I find it odd that my reaction was not, "How the hell did that get here?" but rather, "Hey. A chimp."

I guess I wasn't terribly surprised. Friends leave me disturbing trinkets all the time. Over the years, my buddy Perry gifted me disturbing postcards with dead-eyed dolls, actual dolls (because dolls are creepy), and a papier-mache faceless creature on a small, functioning bicycle. The legs moved when you pushed it. When I called to thank him (my voice full of dubious gratitude), he said, "Isn't it horrible? I wouldn't want it *my* house; I don't think I could sleep with that thing in my house."

Thanks, Perry.

One "treasure" from Perry is bulbous-headed creature that defies description as an animal. Dog? Monkey? Is the thing human? The creature is distressed, using both meanings: it's painted and scraped but also when someone comes upon it suddenly in my house, the thing elicits a reaction of instant repugnance. It's Egyptian-like eyes and slightly twisted un-smile give the wooden creature a sinister demeanor.

About nine years ago, my friend Dave borrowed my power sander and I artfully hid the bulbous-headed thing under sandpaper, hoping to give him a good scare.

Twenty minutes after he left, my phone rang and the first words I heard from Dave's mouth were, "What the hell is wrong with you?"

"What's up?" I asked sweetly.

"I found *that thing* in the bag. The Companion," Dave said.

"The Companion?"

Dave said, "Yes. Its name is The Companion. You *know* that's its name."

Instead of laughing, I recoiled. Of course I had never named the thing, but when he said it aloud, I recognized the truth in his words. He was right. Its name is The Companion.

Now, when houseguests step back and gasp, "What the hell is that?" Truth compels me to say in woeful response, "The Companion."

In teenage horror movies, the first disastrous mistake is to speak aloud an evil thing's true name. You can count on three basic horror movie commands doomed to always be ignored: 1) Don't call the ultimate evil by name and/or read spells from an ancient book, 2) Don't accidentally collect ancient talismans, Egyptian necklaces, voodoo dolls, etc. 3) Don't be a virgin.

Personally, I'm not overly worried about The Companion because I do not collect disturbing artifacts. Plus, I am not a virgin. Okay, well, technically, yes, I'm a virgin. I've never had sex with a woman. But, as a gay man, that kind of virginity doesn't count. Right?

My point is this: my friends are creepy. They say creepy things and mail me creepy stuff and they torture me by leaving it for me in my kitchen cupboards for me to find weeks later, and think, "Hey. A chimp." What's with all these people? I can't find a common denominator. I should probably trash the creepy gifts. I probably shouldn't make space for it in my dining room as I did with The Companion.

I decided my friend Michael (who loves gorillas) is goofy enough to leave me a chimp, so I called and left a snarky voicemail, busting him. Imagine my surprise two days later when well-mannered, bank executive Ron asked during a telephone call, "Did you find anything in your kitchen cupboards lately?"

Over the phone Ron described how pressing a button on the back of its head emits a piercing screech and the chimp's crystal eyes blaze a blinding LED blue light. When I say blinding, what I mean is BLINDING, because for the week after Ron's explanation, I tested it with friends, making them peer into the chimp's crystal eyes while I said, "Watch." I pressed the button and they would jerk their heads away, rubbing their eyes and calling me an asshole.

"I know," I would say excitedly. "It's surprising how strong that little light is. It *really* hurts your eyes, doesn't it?"

That night on the phone, I asked Ron why he gifted me this little creature and he said, "Well, because you collect creepy monkeys."

I gently protested. I had no idea what he meant.

"Well," Ron said, "There's the painted wooden one with the fez and vest on your hutch with all the plants. The big empty eyes."

"That's just one," I said. "It was a gift from Perry, so it doesn't count."

"And the horrible Father Christmas monkey you tried to give away as a prize at your Halloween party. Nobody would touch it because we all assumed it was cursed. Remember?"

Two.

Ron said, "Plus, The Companion. That thing is a monkey, right?"

I got quiet.

When other people experience light bulb moments, I imagine they always see warm, fuzzy, yellow and feel a soft glow of recognition. My light bulb moments always flash dangerously, an orange-flickering Halloween moment right before my brain and mouth say in unison, "Oh fuck."

"*Three* creepy monkeys is a coincidence," I said to Ron. I didn't quite believe him but I found myself growing defensive. "Yes, it's strange—"

At that exact moment, my eyes fell on a gorgeous statuary protecting the fireplace mantle: a Chinese deity known as the Monkey King. The exquisitely carved statue came from San Francisco's Chinatown and is associated with Greg, the best person I met in San Francisco during my five-month visit.

Greg and I met shortly after I moved into a fabulous tree-house apartment and we dated a few times. On our second date, I had a low fever but we *really* wanted to see each other, so we ate take-out from a health food store on a stone bench at the folksy, quiet intersection of Noe and Henry. I felt like crap and Greg made concerned, frowny faces across from me because he felt bad that I felt bad. I remember thinking, "This is why we go on dates. For moments like this."

A lovely moment marred by my inability to lean over and kiss him without risking his health. My sparkling life moments are often tempered by some detail that isn't quite right. It's the ying and yang, I guess. Great joys intertwined with some imperfect detail that throws off the moment.

Although we did not date long, Greg and I developed a sweet friendship that endures to this day. Greg will always have a place of honor in my heart. The Monkey King myth means something special to us. I do not categorize my Monkey King statue on the fireplace mantle as creepy in any way, but he's fierce and poised in attack position, which others might see as disturbing.

With Ron, I remained silent on the phone.

He said, "You found another monkey, didn't you? Did you *honestly* not know that you collect them? Remember the Curious George card you sent me where you explicitly described raunchy, monkey sex—"

I ended the call abruptly.

The next day I shared with Mary-Scott how "Crazy Ron" absurdly thought I collected creepy monkeys after only six data points. Crazy, crazy Ron. Anybody could happen to have a number of unique monkeys in their home and not deem it a collection. I knew Mary-Scott would agree with me.

She said, "Did he count The Companion?"

"Yes," I said, a bit testy.

She said, "And of course, Bongo."

"Bongo?" I said, surprised.

Mary-Scott said, "He didn't know about *Bongo*?"

Bongo is a Beanie Baby I once kept in my office cubicle. He was kidnapped one day by coworker friends, replaced with an anonymous ransom note providing little more than a web address. I visited the website to find Bongo's captivity artfully revealed through a series of photos showing his mouth duct-taped closed and his hands bound together. Captions said things like, "You wouldn't want to see Bongo get hurt, would you?" I met the monkey-napper demands and delivered the required beer to the corporate fridge. Bongo was returned safely.

"He didn't know about Bongo?" Mary-Scott laughed very hard. "What about how you send all those chimp emails with their superimposed creepy voices? Did he know about that?"

I remained silent.

Mary-Scott laughed harder. When she could speak at last, she said, "Surely, *surely* Ron knew about your dad's monkey face, that expression he taught you and your siblings. He knows you can make yourself look like Dr. Zaius, right?"

I remained silent.

As Mary-Scott howled, that orange-flashing bulb smashed itself on and off, that Halloween recognition that perhaps, just *perhaps*, I own a creepy monkey collection.

Later that same night, I discussed this situation with my brother. Together, we remembered a beloved rag doll from my childhood, a monkey, (aptly named Monkey) that I barfed on one midnight while reassuring him that Mom would help us with this stomach ache. My vomit-stained monkey was never seen again. Matt said, "Remember Franco, that monkey finger puppet you made us all pose with? Franco was creepy."

I remained silent.

What's that first rule in teenage horror movies? Don't call an ancient artifact by its true name, bringing it to life. Second rule: don't collect a bunch of creepy talismans that may collectively possess evil powers. The third rule: don't be a virgin.

Oh fuck.

SEX ME UP

SITTING IN my friends' back yard is a slice of Buddhist pie slathered with a Nirvana sauce.

In every direction, I gape. To my left, a meditation corner, stone bench, and fierce orange lilies to guard your quiet thoughts. A melancholy bell groans a desultory clang when a breeze passes through. Ahead of me, the stone-paved fire pit area, surrounded by pinks and purple impatiens. Behind them, yellows daffodils crane forward, eager to be closer to the fire. A nearby metal sculpture of a human face weeps, one of several homemade sculptures throughout the dream landscape. In the back right corner of the garden, a picturesque summer house with cedar shingles and purple trim, French doors, and a secret side entrance obscured by blossoming wisteria.

Snake and his wife Alexis spend uncountable hours creating this sacred space every spring. It's not just pretty, it's potent. I enjoy sitting in their space watching newcomers discover the garden. Noobs gape and say things like, "So beautiful," and "How lovely," but soon all words desert them as the magic takes over, and they fall into silent wonder, touching green leaves in sheer awe, kneeling to let fountain water trickle into their hands as if encountering water outside is somehow miraculous. People adopt stupid, goofy grins while sitting in this garden. I believe in an after-life where we are all happy and loved, because if it didn't exist, how could Snake and Alexis know how create this garden in loving invitation?

Last summer, amidst constant, flowing serenity, I was violated in this garden.

Snake had invited me for an over-due catch-up barbeque, and I arrived Friday night with low-sodium bratwurst and Bing cherries ready to burst. Snake, Alexis and I drank beer near the fire pit surrounded by lusciousness and though I had visited the garden many times before, I could not help but take more photos on my phone. Photos are poor representation of the green bliss, but they would have to do. We discussed death, cancer, and insights gained from sorrow. It may not be common dinner fare, but I am fed well by friends like these.

Sarah, a neighbor friend of theirs, spontaneously joined us. She was built like Summer Fun Barbie, a biologically impossible waist and gravity-defying boobs. She wore a skimpy thin dress, showing off every curve to advantage. Sarah enjoyed telling her experiences selling phone services to prisons, wearing tight clothes to deliberately attract catcalls and whistles from the inmates. While some women (and men) might wish to pass through prison hallways unnoticed, Sarah enjoyed putting on a show and giving the prisoners spank material. After two generous glasses of wine she modeled for us her seductive prison walk. It's possible Sarah had some issues.

"I don't mind," she said, swilling her glass of white wine. "They need a little something."

At Sarah's bidding, Snake retrieved a blanket and hand lotion from the house.

Sarah turned to Alexis and said, "Give me your foot. It's foot massage time."

Oh.

A little unusual appetizer before dinner, but I like to imagine (i.e. self-delude) myself as a go-with-the-flow kinda guy. Sarah's massage surprised Alexis too, and I knew this when our eyes met, mirroring each other's mild alarm. Sarah started with Alexis' feet, yes. But she soon stroked Alexis' calf, her hands skimming higher and higher until slightly above the knee. Rather invasive if you asked me. Alexis said, "Wow," but did not protest any further, so perhaps neighborly affection was different here in Bliss Garden. Back at my place, my neighbors and I just usually gossip over the fence twice a year, not touch each other's thighs with lotion.

After she finished Alexis, Sarah turned to me. "Your turn."

"No thank you," I said. "You don't want to see these feet. Trust me on that."

Sarah said, "I really don't care about the shape your feet are in. It won't bother me."

I declined again.

Sarah insisted. Then, she *insisted*. She dragged a chair in front of me and slapped her knees. "C'mon. Put the left one here."

Yeah, okay. Weird to get foot massaged by Snake and Alexis' neighbor, but okay. I'd submit. This could be another questionable life decision but I do love a good foot massage.

And Sarah was quite good: strong hands, variety of strokes including a few moves that made me groan aloud (which she loved and informed me "inspired her"). She took the same liberties with me she took with Alexis, sliding her hands up my calves and telling me how wonderful they were, how strong. Uh, thanks.

While she massaged me, she explained she volunteered at a retirement home and massaged residents' hands and feet. Shy and reserved individuals opened up soon after she touched them. I considered my discomfort at being massaged by this stranger and then arrived at a new philosophy: fuck it. I was sitting in a Garden of Ease while my very good friend Snake cooked bratwurst and his wife told the fascinating tale of her own adoption secrets revealed. A beautiful woman massaged my feet and rather seemed to enjoy it. Fuck it. Go with this.

Sarah promised me a shoulder massage and my new fuck-it philosophy was called into question. I had hoped the foot massage (with inappropriate calf and thigh flirtation) was the extent of her touch. But she worked my feet a lot longer than Alexis', and I began to worry this massage business wasn't over. I kept thinking of my straight male friends who might enjoy this gorgeous, big-tittied woman slaving over their feet but then I had to wonder, "Wouldn't they think this weird as well?"

Dinner passed quickly amidst laughter and sauerkraut. The very moment I set down my fork, Sarah jumped up from the table and came to stand behind me.

"Time for your neck rub," she said, and yes, I was alarmed.

The way she leapt from the table suggested dinner was an inconvenience to her plans and thank God that was over. I had barely finished chewing. Even Alexis, curled up on a wicker bench with cushions, was alarmed by Sarah's alacrity.

When I heard Sarah rubbing the lotion together in her hands, I tried to relax. Be that go-with-the-flow guy I know lurks inside me. Her hands gripped me well and I could easily admit her skill. Maybe this wouldn't be weird.

Nope. It got weird.

Soon her fingers dipped beneath my shirt and then she unbuttoned the top button for greater access. Snake raised an eyebrow and stared me down as if I were encouraging this. Sarah chatted non-stop through any awkwardness about the tragedy of her mother's mysterious, unexplained death. Meanwhile, her hands sunk into and curled around my chest hair.

"God, I love chest hair," she said and resumed discussing her mother's potential murder.

Were those her big, fleshy boobs pressed against my head? Why, yes, *yes* they were.

Snake refused to make further eye contact with me and found a sudden need to clear dishes from the table.

Snake! Don't leave me! Snake!

Sarah's conversation drifted back to the prison population, then to the elderly she massaged, then to anything, anything that ran through her head. At one point, right before her hands found my nipples she said, "You would not believe the things men in prison say on outgoing phones they *know* are being recorded."

Yes. People can be shocking.

I finally voiced my concern that this massage seemed very, uh, sexual.

"If you want it to be sexual," Sarah said, rubbing my head against her flesh, "it can be."

Alexis could no longer contain herself and started laughing aloud.

I started giggling.

I would swear Sarah was hitting on me except over dinner we discussed my being gay and I know she heard because she said, "My first husband was gay. God, I miss him."

Sarah ratcheted up the dirty talk as her hands passionately caressed my head. "If you feel your cock getting harder, you go right ahead and let it get rock hard."

What?

"Go ahead, baby, go for it," she said, her hands fully inside my shirt, squeezing my chest. "If you need to spurt out a load, you go ahead and let that jizz fly, let it come rocketing out of your cock."

What?

Alexis howled and covered her face with her hands, unable to watch the sex show unfolding before her. And where the hell was Snake?

Sarah continued to molest me, urging me to "shoot that jizz, baby," though honestly, I couldn't have been further from orgasming if I had been masturbating surrounded by nuns in their late 70s. I fancy myself pretty good at raunchy bedroom talk but Sarah's constant stream of insistent demands I blast my semen everywhere—coupled with her impressive mastery of synonyms for ejaculate—proved me a dirty-talk novice. Even I, writer of graphic sexual scenes, couldn't believe the words pouring into my ear and not a single one was meant ironically. No, this was the real deal. I thought I was being punked but it turns out she was trying to convert a gay man, something she could not achieve with her first husband. Well, you couldn't argue she didn't try her best.

Sarah stepped up her aggressive "blow your load" campaign, clenching my skull and whispering directly into my ear. Had I been capable of speech I would have told her to quit, to stop, but my body instinctively curled into the fetal position and I rolled off the garden chair onto the cement tiles, laughing hysterically.

Snake finally returned to find his wife a weeping ball, sobbing and laughing, and me, fetal on the brick patio howling with insane relief, having finally shaken the succubus. Laying on the stone pavement, I could see the tranquil Buddhist garden from a new perspective and I tried to have an insight about Snake and the Garden of Eden, but my brain could only process one question at a time, the most pressing being, "What the fuck just happened here?"

Sarah had refilled her wine glass and said nothing. She sipped her wine. When Snake approached, she said, "You know what I like most about massaging the elderly?"

I remember thinking, "My God. She does this to the elderly!"

I started laughing harder.

FAITH IN BOLINAS

DURING 2008, I lived in San Francisco for a few months. I spent most weekends outside the city, exploring tidal pools, redwood forests and delighting in everything about northern California. One afternoon, while winding my way down the Pacific Coast I lost track of how much gas remained in the tank. In Stinson Beach, I finally took the situation seriously as the gas pump icon blazed with irritation, scolding, "You should know better."

Not too concerned, I pulled over at the surf shop to ask about the nearest gas station.

I asked the shop keep, an older dude (completely a duuuuuuuude) where in town to find the nearest gas station.

Without looking up, he said, "Eleven miles that way."

Older Surfer Dude jerked his finger in the direction I had come.

I clarified that I was looking for the *nearest* gas station.

He pointed again. "Eleven miles."

How about in the other direction?

"Twelve miles."

This is when I began to panic.

I could envision my abandoned Subaru five miles in either direction on twisty, mountainous Highway One, shrugging its hazard lights as if to say, "Hey, he's the one who assumed there'd be gas around here somewhere."

I would be roughly two hundred yards away, bravely trudging the remaining six or seven miles. Around one of those dangerous curves I would become a two-dimensional splat on the grill of a Dodge Caravan, whose driver glanced at the mesmerizing ocean seascape "for only a second." Their entire family would remember The Vacation When Dad Killed a Hitchhiker With Our Rented Minivan.

While I lived out these final moments in my brain, Older Surfing Dude must have overcome his aversion to floundering tourists, because he softened his eyes and looked intently at me.

"There *is* another gas station that's closer," he said. "But it's hard to find."

I insisted that it was my only option. The low-gas warning light had been blinking for several miles already.

His directions were odd. "Drive to the end of the lagoon. Take your first left. Then another left. Then another left. Go a few miles. You'll come to the gas station."

I asked for the names of the roads, but he insisted they were no road signs.

"How can there be no road signs?" I asked.

"There just aren't," he said.

"What's the name of the place where I'm headed?"

"Bolinas," Older Surfer Dude said. "But there won't be any signs for the town."

I studied him, believing this might be some sort of scam. Maybe a buddy of his would trail me and then politely offer to charge me $200 for a ride to the nearest gas station. The strangest part of the story wasn't even the missing road signs.

"A lagoon?" I said.

"Yes, a lagoon."

"A lagoon? With you know, water?"

"Yes. A *lagoon*."

"Next to the ocean. There's a lagoon."

"Right around the curve up there."

I almost said one more time, "Seriously, a lagoon?" but I could tell he grew tired of this repetitious exchange and I wasn't quite ready to call him a liar.

I did mention one more time that if I got lost I was sunk.

He did not tell me how far the gas station was, but reiterated if I kept making left turns around the lagoon, I would be fine.

I left very unsure. How much do you trust strangers? Strangers who were initially surly and unhelpful?

About a half mile south of the surf shop I came upon a marshy swamp with cattails, half-submerged piles of mud. It was expansive. Looked rather deep in some parts. And although adjacent to the ocean, it was cut off from the larger body of water. I guess you'd call it a lagoon. Huh. Whaddaya know.

Then came an intersection with unmarked roads.

I decided what was needed was a bit of faith. I had already driven three miles. Optimistically, my cheerful blue Subaru may have had four more miles in it, tops, with that last half-mile coasting on fumes. But I doubted it.

Still.

I decided to have faith in Bolinas.

Bolinas would be there. Gas would be there.

I turned left on the unnamed road.

The surrounding landscape seemed rural and rugged, scrub trees on brown hills and dilapidated farm houses made me wish I had rented *The Hills Have Eyes* on DVD so at least I'd recognize the signs when they attacked. I had no idea California could get so rural so instantly. Three miles (and one lagoon) back in the direction I came you could shop at Spiritual Books and Gifts, linger over Jerry's Gelato, and visit a sprinkling of exclusive shops catering to driftwood souvenirs.

Faith.

I drove another mile.

Two miles.

Another left turn.

Another mile.

I passed a pumpkin patch and vowed that if I made it to this mythical Bolinas, I'd come back and celebrate by purchasing my Halloween pumpkin. Seeing a pumpkin patch was enormously hopeful, actually. I had come to accept that I would run out of gas any moment now and a friendly pumpkin patch assured me everything would be fine.

Everything. Would. Be. Fine.

Older Surfer Dude had not lied about the directions, the mysterious lack of signage. He did right by me. Everything. Would. Be. Fine.

I traveled another half-mile and the engine spluttered.

And suddenly...Bolinas! The town leapt from behind a small hill of protective trees gleefully shouting, "Here I am."

I coasted into the gas station on fumes.

After my faithful Subaru guzzled his fill, I explored this twelve-building town with no names and no roads. A hand-painted sign for jewelry, pottery, and painting seemed to draw a number of ambulatory tourists in the early Sunday evening.

CRAFTSTMAN TOWN MEETING, yelled a crude sign in front of the small square that must have been the town hall. A corkboard affixed to the exterior of the Bolinas general store was covered with a smattering of announcements including a magician looking for work, an elderly resident who requested that people drive slower through town, and a kid's scrawled plea for "the return of my skateboard, no questions asked."

I returned to the pumpkin patch and picked out my guy. A smallish, cheerful pumpkin, still snoozing nestled amidst its vines, dreaming pumpkin dreams. I was confused by the payment system. Nobody stepped up to take my cash. A few others harvested pumpkins like me, but they didn't appear to work here either.

An older woman with her grandchildren explained, "It's the honor system."

I left my money in a giant metal box bolted to the wagon proclaiming, PUMPKINS HERE, as if the field of bright orange wasn't quite clear. Bolinas saved me and offered me a pumpkin, trusting my honor to make it right. I zoomed back to Highway

One, past the surf shop, the crystal stores, through the zig-zaggy roads back to my tree-house apartment in San Francisco.

I keep trying to attach a moral to my adventure, something about unsought adventures, mystery towns with no signage or the ability to trust strangers. In the end, there is no moral to the story. Just a reminder to have faith in Bolinas.

IS THIS A DREAM?

I HAVE a weird life. Odd shit happens.

But I cringe writing this because when I hear people say "I have a weird life," I almost automatically hate them. They shake their heads sagely, implying it's not easy and takes great personal character to sustain the weirdness.

Ugh. Drama much?

I do not say, "I've had a weird life," to get sympathy or subtly boast about my ability to handle the strange settings I find myself in. No, my life has been a breeze when I hear what others have lived through. I know friends who have dealt with great burdens, harrowing sadness, lives of adversity and sometimes just greater hilarity more than my silly tales.

No, I'm just an idiot. That's not really suffering, that's just, you know, making questionable decisions about your next-door neighbor's Penthouse advances. Not knowing how to handle extremely sexual foot massages or law enforcement officers who say they'd like to see you swing from a rope.

I think we all have weird lives, the way we travel through the day, the way we think about friends, life, experiences. Every story in this book is true, and yet I bet you could write your own book of tales titled, *I Probably Shouldn't Have Done That Either*. Your stories would be different from mine but would covey similar sadness, the same wonder, delicious surprises and horrible misunderstandings. Your flavor, not mine.

I used to think I had a specially blessed life. An astrologer confirmed it once, explaining moons in Jupiter were working overtime for me. I had the lucky moon in the lucky phase in the lucky alignment with a constellation of three Snickers bars (I don't remember the exact details) but in terms of luck it was the equivalent of a diamond inside a diamond wrapped in diamonds.

But the astrologer never exactly specified it was good luck. Maybe it's bad luck, but I don't think so. I wouldn't know so many amazing people if I had bad luck. I wouldn't feel so loved and beautiful if I weren't cared for by the best people on the planet, so based on this empirical evidence, it's clearly not bad luck.

Sometimes I think my weird, lucky life is a dream, a silly, magnificent dream.

And that's wonderful because I dream a lot. I mean, *a lot*. Always did.

Mom tells of my childhood, how I would clomp down stairs from the bedroom I shared with my younger brother and while she cooked eggs or dipped the French toast, I would say, "Want to hear my dreams?" I would elaborate great tales for her, terrible and surprising adventures, stories that rattled her and made her wonder, "How does this kid think like this?" For a little while she worried some unknown adult was influencing me, telling me adult things. She simply didn't understand how a nine-year-old with my limited life experiences could dream so big about lives unknown.

I guess that's what every writer does, dreams of lives unknown.

These days, I sometimes share my dreams on Facebook as I eat my eggs or French toast for breakfast. I share the ones that delight me, fascinate me, scare me a little. But I don't write out every dream and I don't share the significant dreams (the ones clearly about shit I need to work on). I enjoy my public life, but I enjoy my private life even more.

I thought to finish this book of my tales describing one of those beautiful dreams, a significant dream, one that still sings in my heart.

As fate would have it, this very dream also expresses how I feel about my life, the awful, beautiful flannel-and-camo messy conflagration that is Edmond Manning. You may finish these essays thinking, "Thank God I'm not that guy." But I love this weird life of mine, partially because it's so amazingly ordinary, so similar to everyone else's life but also it somehow sparkles just right, just for me.

The Physics Dream

The stars flourished boldly on this warm summer night in the village where I lived, nestled in an almost European countryside. I knew I was a mutant with emerging powers. I could feel them welling up, crackling inside me, ready to explode. I didn't know if I'd be dangerous (i.e. shoot lasers from my eyes, discharge energy bolts of raw power from my fingertips, etc.) so I decided I needed to be alone when my mutant gift emerged. I leapt away from the village, these big, bouncing leaps. I ran and jumped, each leap sending me sailing higher and further than a normal jump should. Gravity didn't apply to me. The night air was fragrant and clean, so crisp it hurt my lungs and I loved it.

In four or five bounds, I cleared the small town and bounced into a forest opening, thick ancient trees dozing everywhere except for a grassy meadow. The dark was darker here, the stars shone brighter. I was filled with jubilation because it was time. *Time*! I was ready to explode!

I jumped straight up into the air, arms spread in expectation and as I drifted higher and higher, I wondered if this was my power, to jump and stay aloft. Up, up, up! Gradually my ascension would pause and I would hover for a few seconds before drifting down, accelerating but not speeding uncomfortably until my feet touched the earth, giving way like a grassy trampoline, enough for me to push up, launching myself even higher. Up, up, up!

I soon cleared the tree tops, hovering in the sky surrounded by pure black and the immeasurable stars. I held out my arms wide to drink every second into me. The air tasted of fresh periwinkle. As I gazed around, I now understood my mutant ability: I could see physics. Colored lights connected stars to other stars, tracing patterns revealing physics phenomenon, big green outlines illuminated laws that were hidden until now. It was breathtaking. I could not form words. I sped to the earth, jumped and bulleted higher into the sky. *Higher*! Looking around, I understood why string theory was accurate but not all the time, why vacuums formed and what was inside black holes. Lights and colors flashed before me, explaining mysteries that I could barely comprehend with my limited brain.

The stars themselves held the key to full understanding. We thought they were pretty, twinkling up there in the sky. Nobody realized that every time someone shook their fist at the sky and yelled, "Why, God, *why*?" they were staring at the ultimate blueprint, the answer to everything. Somehow, we instinctively know to stare at the sky and demand answers.

I did not comprehend most of the revelations, the colors, the outlines, the physics. Hell, I was just some idiot who could jump high and see the patterns. I needed an astrophysicist to listen to my communications. My job wasn't to understand physics, but describe the beauty, the poetry in connections in the underlying architecture. We searched for explanations in the world, but we searched the wrong way. We should have been looking for *beauty* in the world and through beauty, all would be revealed. It seemed to me this was intentional, artists were supposed to pair up with scientists who would apply their methods, integrating the principle of beauty.

I could see the connections fading as I spun in the sky, watching the constellations reveal their grand secrets. As I drifted to earth one last time, I felt complete and loved. It was all about love. I wafted to the ground, forgetting the exact physics revelations, but I knew I could return to them. I could always return to that beauty. Secrets of the universe are always revealed to idiots and storytellers, people who are born under lucky stars.

The dream concluded with a friend finding me in the woods at daybreak. By this point, I was a young woman, roughly eighteen years old. I walked past this friend who said, "You smell like fresh pine," and I smiled broadly because is there anymore more amazing in the world than the smell of fresh pine?

Boy, wasn't that fun? If you enjoyed reading these tales, you might enjoy reading my fiction. Praise for Edmond Manning and *King Perry* (first book in the Lost and Founds series):

"Finally, it comes down to my choice for Best Book of 2012, which goes to the brilliant and beautiful *King Perry* by Edmond Manning. I can say, with all honesty, I've never read a book quite like it in my entire life. Simply put, it is the reason I read and read and read, because every so often I find a book that leaves me both speechless and wanting to shout its praises from the rooftops at the same time. If you haven't read it yet, do. Soon. Like maybe right now, soon. "

Lisa at The Novel Approach,
www.thenovelapproachreviews.com

"This story is so intricate and detailed, the amount of research alone is mind boggling. Details are interwoven and breadcrumbs are dropped that pick up in different places throughout the book in an amazing feat of writing. But despite the complexity of the story, it never gets bogged down and we sail along with Perry and Vin through their amazing weekend journey."

Jay at Joyfully Jay, www.joyfullyjay.com, Best of 2012

"Edmond Manning, bless him, has written a book of rare depth, beauty and importance. This work is all about the pains of the heart, finding ones true self and connecting with the mysteries of life. It is funny yet serious, deep yet easy, and heart breaking yet heartwarming. If read with an open heart, this gem of a book has the power of healing, the serenity of grace, and the security of a father's hug. It's about being powerful and connected and alive."

Tom at A Bear on Books,
tom-webb.blogspot.com (also on his best of 2012 books)

"Edmond Manning is a very good storyteller, one who knows how to draw his reader in, let them wonder what is going on and deliver some plot twists that leaves them going "OH MY!". The writing is tight, characters are very well written, almost that I was expecting to meet them on the corner of my street. For being a debut book, I was literally stunned speechless when I finished it."

Dawn @ Dawn's Reading Nook,
dawnsreadingnook.blogspot.com

ACKNOWLEDGMENTS

My life would be boring without the lovely people all around me. Thank you to Ann Batenburg, Jenna Blum, Snake and Alexis Bloomstrand, Ron Traxinger, Perry Green, Joel Whitehead, Joe McCurdy, my immediate family living and dead: Dad, Mom, Andrea, Eileen, and Matt. Kyle Feldman, Anna Bloomstrand, Stephen Medlicott, Erik Bloomstrand, Rosa Costain, Mike Templeton, Mary-Scott Hunter, Austin Gullixson, Meg Corcoran, Mary Doran, Heather Lewis, the adorzable Logan Lewis-Doran and equally adorzable Cian Lewis-Doran, Tony Ward, the Pink Angels, Christian Khoury, Alesia Tyree, John Wolf, Pat Murphy, and all those who welcomed me into their lives whose names I'm currently blanking. Please know I intend no intentional snubbing through exclusion. I'm just an idiot. I end with a private note to the Bear Walker king, Theo Bishop. Come home, Theo.

ALSO BY
EDMOND MANNING

The Lost and Founds series:
King Perry
King Mai

AWOL, *Men of Honor anthology*

ABOUT THE AUTHOR

EDMOND MANNING has always been fascinated by fiction: how ordinary words could be sculpted into heartfelt emotions, how heartfelt emotions could leave an imprint inside you stronger than the real world. Mr. Manning never felt worthy to seek publication until recently, when he accidentally stumbled into his own writer's voice that fit perfectly, like his favorite skull-print, fuzzy jammies. He finally realized that he didn't have to write like Charles Dickens or Armistead Maupin, two author heroes, and that perhaps his own fiction was juuuuuuust right, because it was his true voice, so he looked around the scrappy word kingdom that he created for himself and shouted, "I'M HOME!" He is now a writer.

In addition to fiction, Edmond enjoys writing nonfiction on his blog, www.edmondmanning.com. When not writing, he can be found either picking raspberries in the back yard or eating panang curry in an overstuffed chair upstairs, reading comic books.

Feel free to contact him at remembertheking@comcast.net.

www.ingramcontent.com/pod-product-compliance
Lightning Source LLC
Chambersburg PA
CBHW060754050426
42449CB00008B/1404